COCKTAILS
HOW TO MIX THEM

by
'ROBERT'

Of the American Bar, Casino Municipal,
Nice
and late of the Embassy Club, London

Martino Publishing
Mansfield Centre, CT
2015

Martino Publishing
P.O. Box 373,
Mansfield Centre, CT 06250 USA

ISBN 978-1-61427-832-0

© 2015 Martino Publishing

Cover design by T. Matarazzo

Printed in the United States of America On 100% Acid-Free Paper

COCKTAILS
HOW TO MIX THEM

by
'ROBERT'

Of the American Bar, Casino Municipal,
Nice
and late of the Embassy Club, London

HERBERT JENKINS LIMITED
3 DUKE OF YORK STREET, ST. JAMES'S
LONDON, S.W.1

MADE AND PRINTED IN GREAT BRITAIN
BY EBENEZER BAYLIS AND SON, LTD., THE
TRINITY PRESS WORCESTER AND LONDON

COCKTAILS
HOW TO MIX THEM

WHAT THIS BOOK IS ABOUT

Hundreds of thousands know how to drink a cocktail; but few can mix one. That was the inception of this book.

Robert is well known as an expert, first at the Royal Automobile Club, then the Criterion, finally at the Embassy Club.

He gives full instructions as to the mixing of all the well-known cocktails, and not only cocktails, but cobblers, coolers, crustas, egg noggs, fizzes, flips, frappés, highballs, juleps, pousse cafés, punches, rickeys, sangarees, slings, smashes, sours and toddies.

Above all, he tells how, with a comparatively trifling expenditure, it is possible to give your friends first-class cocktails at home.

CONTENTS

INTRODUCTION

COCKTAILS were first introduced in America more than a hundred years ago; but their exact origin is rather a mystery. Many stories are told to account for the bulk of the cocktail. The one generally accepted is:

The squire of a little country inn was very proud of his beautiful daughter, and he was equally fond of a magnificent prize-fighting cock. The bird suddenly disappeared and could not be found anywhere. Weary of searching the country round, he swore and told everybody in the village that the man who brought the cock back alive would be allowed to marry his daughter.

Many days passed, until one summer morning a young cavalry officer rode into the village, stopped in front of the inn, and handed the cock back to its owner.

The squire, full of joy, produced drinks that all might toast the tail of the cock, who had not lost a single feather. His daughter, either by accident, or from excitement at the sight of her future husband, mixed whisky, vermouth, bitters and ice together. Everybody liked this delicious concoction so much that it was christened on the spot "Cocktail."

The officer introduced the "cocktail" amongst his fellow officers, and soon it became known to the entire American Army. Gradually its reputation grew, and the cocktail became famous all over the world.

The cocktail habit is now universal. Men started to drink them first, women took to them afterwards, and, as they are more difficult to please, expert mixers had to invent all kinds of new drinks to satisfy the feminine taste. The two wars also helped a great deal to make cocktails popular in England and Europe. Our Canadian friends and American allies wanted their cocktail over here just as in their "own home town," and they are as good judges of cocktails as the Frenchman is of wine, or the Englishman of whisky or beer.

It is stressed in some quarters that excessive cocktail drinking stimulates a false appetite and is ruinous to the health. This is probably quite true, just as any other habit carried to excess will eventually produce ill effects, but it does not mean that cocktails should not be taken in moderation. Indeed they form an excellent stimulant before a meal and leave the palate clean and appreciative.

The mixer, either amateur or professional, should always bear in mind that no standard measures or glasses exist for cocktails and other mixed drinks. The author has adopted certain measures and glasses, the capacities of which are here explained beforehand.

GILL OR NOGGIN. The standard measure adopted in this book is the Gill or Noggin (=0.142 litre), a recognised measure when dealing in wines or spirits. Four gills=one pint=0.568 litre.

The glasses described in the numerous recipes are:

THE COCKTAIL-GLASS, which contains about half a gill of liquid. The mixer should be very careful when ½, ⅓, ¼, ⅕, ⅙ or ⅛ are mentioned in a cocktail recipe; that means ½, ⅓, ¼, etc., of the capacity of the cocktail glass. For instance, a cocktail which is made of half gin and half vermouth has ½ the quantity of a half-gill measure or ¼ gill of gin and ¼ vermouth.

THE WINE-GLASS measures twice as much as a cocktail-glass, that is to say one gill of liquid. The small wine-glass contains ¾ gill of liquid.

THE TUMBLER which is used for long drinks, such as coolers, egg noggs, fizzes, highballs, etc., holds two gills, or half a pint of liquid.

THE LIQUEUR GLASS contains ¼ gill of liquid, but liqueurs are now generally served in a large glass. A cocktail-glass filled up by one-half only is very suitable.

THE POUSSE CAFÉ GLASS holds ¾ gill of liquid.

THE CRUSTA GLASS is similar in size to the small wine-glass.

THE MINT JULEP GLASS is a large glass shaped like a bowl; it holds half a pint.

It is also necessary to explain a few terms adopted in this work:

STIR UP A DRINK means mixing the drink with a long, thin spoon (bar spoon) by whirling it round smartly until the ingredients are absolutely cold. This is generally done in the bar glass, a tall and thick glass with a strong bottom. Some mixing glasses fit the shaker, others have a lip for pouring-out purposes and to avoid spilling the liquors.

SHAKE A DRINK means fastening the shaker into the bar glass or the two nickel receptacles one into the other. Hold in both hands and shake up and down until the ingredients are properly mixed and cold enough.

To STRAIN A DRINK, fit the strainer into the mouth of the bar glass or shaker, and pour the drink into the serving glass, holding back the ice. Some shakers have a strainer fitted in the top; but they are not to be recommended, the straining taking too much time.

To SQUEEZE LEMON PEEL on top, take a piece of lemon peel, twist it between the fingers over the drink to extract the oil and throw the peel aside. The lemon peel should only be put in the glass when specially required, and also in a few drinks where mentioned in this book. Some mixers prefer squeezing the lemon peel in the glass before pouring the ingredients into it; this is merely a matter of taste.

A DASH OF BITTERS is equal to ⅛ of a teaspoonful. There are between 16 and 18 teaspoonfuls in a cocktail glass (⅛ gill measure).

When mixing drinks there are certain things that should always be remembered:

1. Use clean ice, and handle with the ice scoop. Artificial ice is more economical than natural ice, it is not so slimy and keeps clear.

2. Use the best brands of liqueurs. It is impossible to mix a good drink when using materials of poor quality.

3. Minerals should be kept cold enough to be served without ice. Syphons should never be kept on ice, as they may explode when subjected to a sudden change of temperature.

4. Use plain Syrup, that is Sugar Syrup, or even Gum Syrup, in preference to powdered sugar. The Syrup mixes better with the drink. It should, however, be borne in mind that certain drinks are always prepared with sugar, i.e. the old-fashioned cocktail, the Champagne Cocktail, the Collins', etc.

5. Bitters, Cordials and Syrups should be used with the greatest care. A little too much changes the entire taste of a drink, spoiling instead of improving it as it should do. They should be kept in a moderate temperature, but not put on ice. Care should be taken to prevent insects from entering the mixing bottles. When using the mixing bottles (also called bitter bottles) keep one

finger on the stopper to prevent it dropping into the mixing glass or shaker.

6. Fruits and fruit juice should be kept cool to preserve their freshness. Fruits cut in slices should be handled with a fork, and when used for ornament in a drink they should be placed on the top in a tasteful manner, then add a spoon and straws.

7. When using eggs for drinks, always break the egg in the shaker first, or in a separate glass to make sure it is fresh, and thus avoid spoiling a mixture already prepared.

8. Milk used for mixing drinks should be rich, and never boiled beforehand.

9. While mixing always bear in mind the right ingredients, and the exact proportions. Most bartenders start by putting the ice in the mixing glass, or shaker first; then come the bitters, fruit juice, egg and the liqueurs (the heavier ones first). It really matters little in what order the ingredients have been put into the shaker, as they are all well stirred up or shaken before being strained into the glass and served.

Utensils

The professional mixer of cocktails who produces hundreds in the day requires the following utensils, which should always be at hand:

1. A ½ gill, a ¼ gill, a ⅓ gill and also, if possible, a ⅙ gill measure.

2. A mixing or bar glass and a mixing spoon.

3. A shaker, that is to say a pair of nickel receptacles which fit one into the other. (The bar glass should also fit into the larger receptacle.)

4. A strainer with a sprig that fits into the mixing glass and the shaker.

5. Five decanter bottles with stoppers filled with:

Orange Bitters.
Angostura Bitters.
Brown Curaçao.
Absinthe.
Plain or Gum Syrup.

Sometimes a sixth Bitter decanter is filled with Grenadine or Raspberry according to necessity.

6. A lemon knife and a squeezer.

7. A muddler to crush sugar, fruit and mint.

8. A corkscrew and a mineral-water opener.

9. A machine to chop the ice, an ice pick, and a scoop or tongs to handle the ice.

10. A fork and spoon for handling fruit.

11. Straws and wooden picks for cherries and olives put in the cocktail-glasses.

12. A nutmeg grater, salt, red pepper, vinegar, tomato ketchup, Worcester sauce, eggs, milk, lemons, oranges, fruit according to season, and sugar.

The amateur can do quite well with numbers 1, 2, 3, 4. The other necessary utensils can be found in any ordinary kitchen.

The Cocktail at Home

Many people wish to enjoy at home what they have enjoyed out—but how? Some guidance and instruction are obviously desirable, and to provide these in simple terms is the purpose of this book.

It is possible to perfect quite a good selection of excellent cocktails at home. To assist the amateur mixer, I give a few hints. For one thing no one desires to fit up a bar at the end of his dining-room, consequently I indicate what may be done with comparatively few bottles of materials.

The "gentleman mixer" should keep on his sideboard:

1. A bottle of Dry Gin of superior quality.
2. A bottle of matured Scotch Whisky.
3. A bottle of good Cognac Brandy.
4. A bottle of mild, Pale Sherry.
5. A bottle of best French Vermouth.
6. A bottle of Italian Vermouth.
7. A small bottle of Angostura Bitters.
8. A small bottle of Orange Bitters.
9. A bottle of plain Sugar Syrup, Gomme or Orgeat.
10. A bottle of Orange Syrup.
11. A bottle of Grenadine or Raspberry Syrup.

Eleven items may look formidable, but it is possible to get along reasonably well if one or more of the less important are not available. Nevertheless, the list tabulated above does form the foundation to a wide variety of drinks. Orange Syrup is a substitute for Curaçao; Sugar Syrup or Gomme should be used in preference to Sugar.

If lemons, oranges, tangerines, pineapple (tinned), mint, eggs, milk, cream and soda water are available, the field is enormously widened and will permit of such excellent concoctions as the: Bamboo, Bennett, Blenton, Brandy, Bronx, Clover Club, Clover Leaf, Cooperstown, Diabolo, Gibson, Harvard, H.P.W., Houla-Houla, Inca, Old-Fashioned, Orange Blossom, Perfect, Queen's, R.A.C., Rob Roy, Royal Clover Club, Spanish, Sunshine, Thistle, Tipperary, Trocadero, Velocity,

X.Y.Z., Yellow Rattler and Wax Cocktails, besides various kinds of cobblers, cups, egg noggs, flips, fizzes, etc., etc.

Although I call this book *Cocktails: How to Mix Them*, I have included particulars as to the preparation of many other drinks, such as cobblers, coolers, crustas, cups, daisies, egg noggs, fizzes, flips, frappés, French apéritifs, highballs, invalid drinks, juleps, lemonades, pousse cafés, punches, rickeys, sangarees, slings, smashes, sours, toddies, etc.

ROBERT VERMEIRE.

COCKTAILS
HOW TO MIX THEM

COCKTAILS

Absinthe

THE art of mixing Absinthe is probably one of the most subtle and least understood.

We have the American style, the French style, the Swiss style.

Absinthe—American Style

The Americans are very fond of the Absinthe Cocktail and the American Absinthe. The best way to make an Absinthe Cocktail is as follows: Fill the shaker half full of broken ice and add:

1 dash of Angostura Bitters.
3 or 4 dashes of plain Syrup or Anisette.
$\frac{1}{4}$ gill of Absinthe.
$\frac{1}{4}$ gill of water.

Shake these ingredients until frozen, strain into a cocktail-glass and squeeze the essence of a little lemon-peel on top.

To make an American Absinthe: Fill the shaker half full with broken ice, add:

$\frac{1}{2}$ gill of Absinthe Pernod.
$1\frac{1}{2}$ gills of plain water.
A little Sugar Syrup according to taste

Shake thoroughly and strain into a tumbler.

Some people shake the Absinthe without the water and strain it into a tumbler, adding cold Soda Water instead.

Absinthe—French Style

It is superfluous to explain here the old-fashioned French way of mixing Absinthe, because the real Absinthe glasses are now absolutely unobtainable.

Just before Absinthe was prohibited in France, it was usually mixed as follows:

Put into a good-sized tumbler, ½ gill of Absinthe, 1 lump of ice, and put across the top of the glass the Absinthe-spoon with 1 or 2 lumps of sugar on it according to taste (the Absinthe-spoon is a flat spoon with plenty of little holes in it). Now pour, drop by drop, water on the sugar. The water dropping through the Absinthe-spoon melts the sugar and sweetens the drink at the same time.

When the glass is full, stir up slightly with the spoon, and your drink is ready. The French amateur Absinthe drinker usually takes 15 to 20 minutes to finish this wonderful stimulator.

Absinthe—Swiss Style

This is the most simple way:

Put ½ gill of Absinthe in a tumbler, add a little plain Syrup, Grenadine, or Anisette, and fill up the balance with iced water.

This drink is also very popular in France and Italy. When Grenadine is used it is generally called *une purée*, or *une tomate*, because its colour is similar to that of a tomato. When plain Syrup is used it is called *mominette* by the French working-man.

Angler Cocktail

This cocktail is very popular in Bohemia and Czecho-Slovakia. It was introduced by V. P. Himmelreich. The ingredients are put in the mixing glass with broken ice:

2 dashes of Angostura Bitters.
2 dashes of Orange Bitters.
¼ gill of Vantogrio (a local non-alcoholic Syrup).
⅜ gill of Gin.

Stir up with the spoon. Strain into a cocktail-glass. Squeeze lemon-peel on top.

Apple Jack Cocktail

In the large bar glass, half full of broken ice, add:

1 or 2 dashes of Angostura Bitters.
2 or 3 dashes of Gum Syrup or Curaçao.
½ gill of Apple Jack Brandy.

Stir up well with mixing spoon, strain into a cocktail-glass, add olive or cherry and squeeze the essence of a lemon-peel on top.

In the U.S.A. Apple Jack Brandy is also called Jersey Lightning. In France they usually call it Calvados.

Bacardi Cocktail

Fill the shaker half full of broken ice, and add:

⅛ gill of fresh Lime Juice.
⅜ gill of Bacardi.
Sugar Syrup according to taste.

Shake well and strain into a cocktail-glass.

When no limes handy, lemons are usually taken instead.

This cocktail is in great demand in London. In the U.S.A. it is undoubtedly more popular than any other cocktail.

Bamboo Cocktail

Fill the large bar glass half full of broken ice and add:

1 dash of Orange Bitters.
¼ gill of Dry Pale Sherry.
¼ gill of French Vermouth.

Stir up well, strain into a cocktail-glass, and squeeze lemon-peel on top.

This drink is very popular amongst the British residents in India, and is also called "Reform Cocktail."

Bennett Cocktail

Fill the shaker half full of broken ice and add:

2 dashes of Angostura Bitters.
⅜ gill of Old Tom Gin.
⅛ gill of fresh Lime Juice.

Shake well and strain into a cocktail-glass.

This cocktail, which is very popular in Chili, is called after the well-known and popular land-owner and millionaire of that country.

Bijou Cocktail

Fill the bar glass half full of broken ice and add:

1 dash of Orange Bitters.
⅓ gill of Plymouth Gin.
⅓ gill of Italian Vermouth.
⅓ gill of Green Chartreuse.

Stir up with a spoon, strain into a cocktail-glass, add olive or cherry according to taste, and squeeze lemon-peel on top.

Blackthorn Cocktail

The Blackthorn is a very old cocktail, which is made in two different ways:
Fill a bar glass half full of broken ice and add:

3 dashes of Absinthe.
3 dashes of Angostura Bitters.
¼ gill of French Vermouth.
¼ gill of Irish Whisky.

Stir well with a spoon, strain into a cocktail-glass, and squeeze lemon-peel on top.

(*Recipe by Harry Johnson, of New Orleans.*)

The cocktail is made in a similar way, but the ingredients are:

1 dash of Orange Bitters.
1 dash of Angostura Bitters.
⅓ gill of Sloe Gin.
⅓ gill of French Vermouth.
⅓ gill of Italian Vermouth.

(*Recipe by "Cocktail Boothby," of San Francisco.*)

Blenton Cocktail

This cocktail is well-known amongst the officers of the British Navy. The ingredients are stirred up in the mixing glass and strained into a cocktail-glass:

¼ gill of Plymouth Gin.
¼ gill of French Vermouth.
1 dash of Angostura Bitters.

No lemon squeezed on top.

Bloodhound Cocktail

Fill the shaker half full of broken ice, and add:

6 nice raspberries.
½ teaspoonful of Maraschino.
⅙ gill of Dry Gin.
⅙ gill of French Vermouth.
⅙ gill of Italian Vermouth.

Shake well and strain into a cocktail-glass. Care should be taken to avoid the pips passing through the strainer into the cocktail-glass.

Remember a cocktail-glass holds ½ a gill (3/6) of liquid.

Boomerang Cocktail

This popular South African drink is made in the large bar glass, half full of broken ice, to which the following ingredients have been added:

2 dashes of Maraschino.
1 dash of Angostura Bitters.
⅙ gill of Gin.
⅙ gill of French Vermouth.
⅙ gill of Italian Vermouth.

Stir up well, strain into a cocktail-glass, add a cherry and lemon-peel squeezed on the top.

Brandy Cocktail

Fill the bar glass half full of broken ice and add:

1 or 2 dashes of Angostura Bitters.
3 dashes of Curaçao.
½ gill of Brandy.

Stir up well, strain into a cocktail-glass, add olive or cherry, and squeeze lemon-peel on top. A little dash of Absinthe improves this cocktail, which is also often made with equal parts of Brandy and French Vermouth. It should be noted that all plain cocktails are made the same way as the Brandy Cocktail. The base liquor can be either Gin, Whisky, Rum, Vermouth, Sherry, etc., and the cocktail is therefore named according to the base liquor.

Brazil Cocktail

The Brazil Cocktail is a Bamboo Cocktail with 2 dashes of plain Syrup and 2 dashes of Absinthe in it.

Bronx Cocktail

Fill the shaker half full of broken ice and add:

The juice of a quarter of an orange.
½ gill of Dry Gin.
⅛ gill of French Vermouth.
¼ gill of Italian Vermouth.

Shake well and strain into a cocktail-glass. Some bar-tenders also add a little dash of Orange Bitters.

This cocktail is named after the well-known New York Zoo. It can also be made with tangerines instead of oranges.

Champagne Cocktail

In a wine-glass put 1 lump of sugar, soak it with Angostura Bitters, squeeze the essence of 2 or 3 pieces of lemon-peel in the glass, and 1 lump of ice, and fill the glass with iced champagne. Stir up slightly with the mixing spoon, squeeze and drop another piece of lemon-peel in the glass.

Note that a bottle of Champagne makes from 5 to 6 cocktails.

Chicago Cocktail

The Chicago Cocktail is also called "Fancy Brandy Cocktail." It is a plain Brandy Cocktail, with a little Champagne on the top, and the squeezed lemon-peel dropped in the glass. Before straining the mixture into the cocktail-glass, moisten the outside borders of the glass with Lemon Juice and dip into pulverised sugar.

Chinese Cocktail

Fill the bar glass half full of broken ice and add:

1 or 2 dashes of Angostura Bitters.
3 dashes of Maraschino.
3 dashes of Curaçao.
3 dashes of Grenadine.
¼ gill of Jamaica Rum.

Stir up well, strain into a cocktail-glass, add a cherry, and squeeze lemon-peel on top.

Chocolate Cocktail

Fill the shaker half full of broken ice and add:

The yolk of a fresh egg.

$\frac{1}{4}$ gill of Yellow Chartreuse.

$\frac{1}{4}$ gill of Port.

1 teaspoonful of sweet powdered chocolate.

Shake well and strain into a small wine-glass. This drink is very well known in Brazil.

Clover Club Cocktail

Fill the shaker half full of broken ice and add:

The white of a fresh egg.

The juice of a small fresh Lime.

1 teaspoonful of Raspberry Syrup.

$\frac{2}{6}$ gill of Gin.

$\frac{1}{6}$ gill of French Vermouth.

Shake well and strain into a small wine-glass. When no limes are to hand, lemons are usually used, and Grenadine is often substituted for Raspberry Syrup.

The Royal Clover Club is made with the yolk instead of the white of egg.

The Clover Leaf is a Clover Club shaken up with 1 or 2 sprigs of fresh mint and decorated with a mint leaf on the top.

Club Cocktail

Fill the bar glass half full of broken ice and add:

1 or 2 dashes of Angostura.

3 dashes of Grenadine.

$\frac{1}{2}$ gill of Whisky.

Stir up with the mixing spoon, strain into a cocktail-glass, add a cherry and squeeze lemon-peel on top.

Coffee Cocktail

The Coffee Cocktail, also called "Law's Cocktail," is made with:

The yolk of a new-laid egg.
1 teaspoonful of Sugar Syrup.
⅛ gill of Brandy.
⅜ gill of Port.

Shake these ingredients well with ice and strain into a small wine-glass with grated nutmeg on top.

Cooperstown Cocktail

The Cooperstown is a Martini Cocktail shaken up with 2 sprigs of fresh mint.

This drink is very popular amongst the cowboys in America. The recipe was given to me by a well-known member of the Peerage who lived amongst them for some time.

Cornwell Cocktail

Fill the shaker half full of broken ice, and add:

⅛ gill of Seville Orange Bitters.
⅜ gill of Dry Gin.

Shake well, strain into a cocktail-glass, put the peel of an olive in the glass, and squeeze lemon-peel on top.

This drink has a delicious orange flavour which is peculiar to the Seville orange out of which the Seville Orange Bitters is made.

Coronation Cocktail

Fill the bar glass half full of broken ice and add:

1 or 2 dashes of Peppermint.
1 or 2 dashes of Peach Bitters.
3 dashes of Curaçao.
½ gill of Brandy.

Stir up well with a spoon, strain into a cocktail-glass, and serve with lemon-peel squeezed on top.

Daïquiri

Daïquiri is the well-known iron mine situated in the southern part of Cuba. The Daïquiri Cocktail is well known in Cuba and the Southern States of the U.S.A.

Fill the shaker half full of broken ice and add:

⅜ gill of Bacardi.
⅛ gill of fresh Lime Juice.
Sweeten with Grenadine.

Shake well and strain into a cocktail-glass.

Deep Sea Cocktail

This Californian drink must be well shaken and iced. It is made of:

¼ gill of Old Tom Gin.
¼ gill of French Vermouth.
1 dash of Orange Bitters.
1 dash of Absinthe.

Strain into a cocktail-glass, add an olive and squeeze lemon-peel on the top.

Dempsey Cocktail

Fill the shaker half full of broken ice and add:

2 dashes of Absinthe.
1 teaspoonful of Grenadine.
$\frac{1}{8}$ gill of Gin.
$\frac{2}{8}$ gill of Calvados.

Shake well and strain into a cocktail-glass.

This drink was introduced at Deauville, 1921, after Dempsey's victory over Carpentier.

Depth Bomb Cocktail

Fill the shaker half full of broken ice and add:

$\frac{1}{4}$ gill of Brandy.
$\frac{1}{4}$ gill of Apple Jack Brandy.
1 teaspoonful of Grenadine.
2 teaspoonfuls of fresh Lemon Juice.

Shake well and strain into a cocktail-glass.

This drink was very popular in the Royal Air Force of the British Empire during the Great War. It is called after the famous bomb which was dropped from the bombarding air machines that caused panic amongst the German troops behind the lines.

Derby Cocktail

This cocktail is made exactly in the same way as the "East India Cocktail," but a dash of Champagne is added before serving.

Devil's Cocktail

Fill the shaker half full with broken ice and add:

¼ gill of Cognac Brandy.
¼ gill of Crème de Menthe (green).

Shake well and strain into a cocktail-glass. Add a pinch of red pepper on the top.

Diabolo Cocktail

Fill the bar glass half full of broken ice and add:

1 or 2 dashes of Angostura.
3 dashes of Orange Curaçao.
¼ gill of Brandy.
¼ gill of French Vermouth.

Stir up with a spoon, strain into a cocktail-glass, and squeeze lemon-peel on top; add cherry or olive to taste.

This cocktail is also known as a "Young Man."

Diki-Diki

Fill the shaker half full of broken ice and add:

¼ gill of Calvados.
⅛ gill of Caloric Punch.
⅛ gill of Grape Fruit Juice.

Shake well and strain into a cocktail-glass.

Diki-Diki is the chief monarch of the Island Ubian (Southern Philippines), who is now 37 years old, weighs 23 lb., and his height is 32 in.

The author introduced this cocktail at the Embassy Club in London, February, 1922.

Diplomate Cocktail

Fill a bar glass half full of broken ice and add:

2 dashes of Maraschino.
$\frac{2}{6}$ gill of French Vermouth.
$\frac{1}{6}$ gill of Italian Vermouth.

Stir up well, strain into a cocktail-glass, add a cherry and squeeze lemon-peel on top. This drink is very well known in the French Diplomatic Service.

Doctor's Cocktail

Fill the shaker half full of broken ice and add:
$\frac{1}{8}$ gill of fresh Lemon Juice.
$\frac{1}{8}$ gill of Orange Juice.
$\frac{1}{4}$ gill of Caloric Punch.
Shake well and strain into a cocktail-glass.

Dubonnet Cocktail*

The Dubonnet Cocktail, formerly called "Zaza Cocktail," includes:
$\frac{1}{4}$ gill of Gin.
$\frac{1}{4}$ gill of Dubonnet.

Stir up in ice, strain into a cocktail-glass, and squeeze orange-peel on top.

When desired dry, use $\frac{2}{6}$ gill of Gin and $\frac{1}{6}$ gill of Dubonnet instead of equal parts.

In San Francisco the Dubonnet Cocktail is made differently. Its ingredients are:

3 dashes of Orange Bitters.
$\frac{2}{6}$ gill of Dubonnet.
$\frac{1}{6}$ gill of Dry Pale Sherry.

* Dubonnet is one of the best-known appetisers in the world. It is not only used for cocktails but also as a cooler and highball.

Stir up well, strain into a cocktail-glass, with a cherry and lemon-peel squeezed on top.

Another Cocktail made with Dubonnet which is very popular in London just now includes:

1 dash of Orange Bitters.
1 dash of Angostura Bitters.
⅙ gill of Dubonnet.
¼ gill of Sherry.
¼ gill of French Vermouth.
Orange-peel squeezed on top.

East India Cocktail

Fill a large bar glass half full of broken ice and add:

2 dashes of Angostura Bitters.
2 dashes of Curaçao.
2 dashes of Maraschino or Pine-apple Syrup.
½ gill of Brandy.

Stir up well, strain into a cocktail-glass, add a cherry, and squeeze lemon-peel on top.

Fairbank Cocktail

Fill the bar glass half full of broken ice and add:

2 dashes of Noyau Rose.
2 dashes of Orange Bitters.
¼ gill of Gin.
¼ gill of French Vermouth.

Stir up well, strain into a cocktail-glass, and squeeze orange-peel on top.

This drink is called after Senator Fairbank, a personal friend of the late President Roosevelt, of America.

Fernet Cocktail

Fill the bar glass half full of broken ice and add:

    1 dash of Angostura Bitters.
    2 dashes of plain Sugar or Gum Syrup.
    ¼ gill of Fernet Branca.
    ¼ gill of Cognac Brandy, or Rye Whisky
        to taste.

Stir up well with a spoon, strain into a cocktail-glass, and squeeze lemon-peel on top.

This cocktail is much appreciated by the Canadians of Toronto.

Fioupe Cocktail

Fill the mixing glass half full of broken ice and add:

    ¼ gill of Italian Vermouth.
    ¼ gill of Cognac Brandy.
    1 teaspoonful of Bénédictine.

Stir up with a spoon, strain into a cocktail-glass, and add cherry, squeeze lemon-peel on top.

Monsieur Fioupe is a familiar figure known all along the Riviera, by everybody, from prince to cabman.

Gibson Cocktail

The Gibson Cocktail is well known in Japan, principally in Yokohama. It is a Martini Cocktail with a tiny white onion in it.

Glad Eye

Fill the shaker half full of broken ice and add:

    ⅔ gill of Absinthe Pernod.
    ⅓ gill of Peppermint Get.

Shake until frozen and strain into a cocktail-glass.

Gloom Raiser

This drink was first introduced by the author of this book at the Royal Automobile Club, 1915. The ingredients, which should be stirred up, are:

⅛ gill of Dry Gin.
⅛ gill of Vermouth Noilly Prat.
2 dashes of Grenadine.
2 dashes of Absinthe.

Squeeze lemon-peel on top.

Handicap Cocktail

Fill the bar glass half full of broken ice and add:

¼ gill of Grand Marnier.
1 wine-glass of Fruchtschaumwein.

Stir up well, strain into a wine-glass, and add a slice of lemon on the top.

This cocktail is well known in Dresden. Fruchtschaumwein is a sparkling lemonade flavoured with fruit juice.

Harvard Cocktail

Fill a bar glass half full of broken ice and add:

2 dashes of Angostura Bitters.
1 dash of Gum Syrup.
¼ gill of Brandy.
¼ gill of Italian Vermouth.

Stir up well, strain into a cocktail-glass, and add lemon-peel squeezed on top.

H.P.W. Cocktail

This cocktail was invented by the famous bar-tender "Charlie," of the Racket Club in New York, as a compliment to the prominent millionaire member of the Club, Mr. Harry Payne Whitney. Ingredients:

$\frac{1}{6}$ gill of Gin.
$\frac{2}{6}$ gill of Italian Vermouth.
1 slice of an orange.

Shake well and strain into a cocktail-glass.

Houla-Houla Cocktail

Fill the shaker half full of broken ice and add:

$\frac{2}{6}$ gill of Gin.
$\frac{1}{6}$ gill of Orange Juice.
1 teaspoonful of Curaçao.

Shake well and strain into a cocktail-glass.
This drink originates from Hawaii.

Inca Cocktail

Fill the bar glass half full of broken ice and add:

2 dashes of Orgeat Syrup.
2 dashes of Orange Bitters.
$\frac{1}{6}$ gill of Plymouth Gin.
$\frac{1}{6}$ gill of French Vermouth.
$\frac{1}{6}$ gill of Dry Pale Sherry.

Stir up well, strain into a cocktail-glass, and add a small piece of pine-apple. Squeeze a little orange-peel on top.

This cocktail was invented by H. C. Harrison, who supervises the American bars of the Gordon Hotels in England.

Jack Rose Cocktail

The Jack Rose ingredients are:

¼ gill of fresh Lime Juice.
A little Raspberry Syrup or Grenadine.
⅝ gill of Apple Jack Brandy.

This drink should be well shaken. Substitute fresh Lemon Juice for Lime Juice when no limes handy.

Klondyke Cocktail

Fill the bar glass half full of broken ice and add:

3 dashes of Orange Bitters.
¼ gill of French Vermouth.
¼ gill of Apple Jack Brandy.

Stir up well, strain into a cocktail-glass, add a small olive, and squeeze lemon-peel on top.

London Cocktail

Fill a bar glass half full of broken ice and add:

2 dashes of Orange Bitters.
2 dashes of Gum Syrup.
2 dashes of Absinthe.
½ gill of London Dry Gin.

Stir up, strain into a cocktail-glass, add an olive, and squeeze lemon-peel on top.

Luigi Cocktail

Fill the shaker half full of broken ice and add:

1 teaspoonful of Grenadine.
1 little dash of Cointreau.
The juice of half a tangerine.
¼ gill of Gin.
¼ gill of French Vermouth.

Shake well and strain into a cocktail-glass.

This cocktail was invented by Mr. Luigi Naintré, the proprietor of the Embassy Club, who became famous at Romano's, Ciro's, and the Criterion. He is one of the best-known *restaurateurs* in the world and has an enormous and faithful following wherever he goes.

This cocktail is one of the most popular in London.

Manhattan Cocktail

Fill a bar glass half full of broken ice and add:

1 or 2 dashes of Angostura Bitters.
2 or 3 dashes of Gum Syrup or Curaçao.
¼ gill of Rye Whisky.
¼ gill of Italian Vermouth.
1 dash of Absinthe if required.

Stir up well, strain into a cocktail-glass, add cherry, and squeeze lemon-peel on top.

This is a very old, but still one of the best-known cocktails, called after the district in New York.

When required dry, use French Vermouth instead of Italian Vermouth. When desired medium, use:

¼ gill of Rye.
⅛ gill of French Vermouth.
⅛ gill of Italian Vermouth.

Martinez Cocktail

The Martinez Cocktail is very similar to the Manhattan Cocktail, but Gin is used instead of Whisky.

Fill the bar glass half full of broken ice and add:

2 dashes of Orange Bitters.
3 dashes of Curaçao or Maraschino.
¼ gill of Old Tom Gin.
¼ gill of French Vermouth.

Stir up well, strain into a cocktail-glass, add olive or cherry to taste, and squeeze lemon-peel on top.

This drink is very popular on the Continent.

In England the Martinez Cocktail generally contains the following ingredients:

2 dashes of Orange Syrup.
2 dashes of Angostura Bitters.
¼ gill of Plymouth Gin.
¼ gill of French Vermouth.

The whole stirred up in ice in the bar glass, strained into a cocktail-glass with lemon-peel squeezed on top. Olive or cherry according to taste.

Third Degree

The Third Degree is a Martinez Cocktail (Continental style) with a dash of Absinthe and an olive, but $\frac{2}{6}$ gill of Gin and $\frac{1}{6}$ gill of French Vermouth should be used.

Fourth Degree

The Fourth Degree is a Martinez Cocktail (Continental style) with a dash of Absinthe and a cherry, but ¼ gill of Gin, $\frac{1}{8}$ gill of French Vermouth, $\frac{1}{8}$ gill of Vermouth should be used.

Rosington

Fill the shaker half full of broken ice and add:

$\frac{2}{8}$ gill of Dry Gin.
$\frac{1}{8}$ gill of Italian Vermouth.
A piece of orange-peel.

Shake well, strain into a cocktail-glass, and squeeze orange-peel on top.

In certain parts of U.S.A. this drink is known as "Roselyn."

Martini Cocktail

Here is the exact recipe:
Fill the bar glass half full with broken ice and add:

1 dash of Orange Bitters.
$\frac{1}{8}$ gill of Italian Vermouth.
$\frac{2}{8}$ gill of Dry Gin.

Stir up and strain into a cocktail-glass. Squeeze lemon-peel on top.

Medium Martini

The Medium Martini Cocktail is a Martini Cocktail made with:

$\frac{1}{4}$ gill of Gin.
$\frac{1}{8}$ gill of Italian Vermouth.
$\frac{1}{8}$ gill of French Vermouth.

Sweet Martini

The Sweet Martini Cocktail is a Martini Cocktail made with:

¼ gill of Italian Vermouth.

¼ gill of Gin.

Note.—The Martini Cocktail should be prepared in the mixing glass and stirred up. In America, however, it has been the fashion, since a few years, to shake this cocktail until thoroughly cold.

Mayfair Cocktail

Fill the shaker half full of broken ice and add:

¼ gill of Dry Gin.

¼ gill of plain Orange Juice.

3 or 4 dashes of Apricot Syrup flavoured with a little Cloves Syrup.

Shake well and strain into a cocktail-glass. This cocktail possesses a delicious flavour. I invented it at the Embassy Club in London, 1921. Mayfair is the aristocratic quarter of London, called so because under the reign of Charles II (seventeenth century) they used to hold a yearly fair there during the month of May.

Meehoulong

Fill the bar glass half full of broken ice and add:

1 dash of Orange Bitters.

¼ gill of Sloe Gin.

⅛ gill of French Vermouth.

⅛ gill of Italian Vermouth.

Stir up with a spoon, strain into a cocktail-glass, and squeeze lemon-peel on top.

Meehoulong is the Chinese word for "fire-eating devil."

Mikado Cocktail

Fill the bar glass half full of broken ice and add:

2 dashes of Angostura Bitters.
2 dashes of Noyau.
2 dashes of Orgeat.
2 dashes of Curaçao.
½ gill of Cognac Brandy.

Stir up well, strain into a cocktail-glass, add a cherry, and squeeze lemon-peel on top.

This cocktail is also called "Japanese Cocktail."

Millionaire

Fill the shaker half full of broken ice and add:

The white of a fresh egg.
2 dashes of Curaçao.
⅛ gill of Grenadine.
⅞ gill of Rye Whisky.

Shake well and strain into a small wine-glass. A dash of Absinthe may be added if required.

This cocktail is well known to the patrons of the Ritz Hotel, London.

Monkey's Gland Cocktail

Fill the shaker half full of broken ice and add:

2 teaspoonfuls of Absinthe.
2 teaspoonfuls of Grenadine.
¼ gill of Gin.
¼ gill of fresh Orange Juice.

Shake well and strain into a cocktail-glass.

This cocktail is very popular in Deauville and London. Harry MacElhone, the well-known bartender of Ciro's Club, invented it.

Morning Cocktail

Fill the bar glass half full of broken ice and add:

2 dashes of Curaçao.
2 dashes of Maraschino.
2 dashes of Orange Bitters.
2 dashes of Absinthe.
¼ gill of Brandy.
¼ gill of French Vermouth.

Stir up and strain into a cocktail-glass, add a cherry and lemon-peel twisted on top.

Midnight Cocktail

This cocktail used to be very much appreciated amongst the dancing people at the Savoy Hotel in London a few years ago. It is a Bronx Cocktail shaken up with a dash of Absinthe.

In China this cocktail is known as the *Minnehaha Cocktail*, but the Absinthe is poured in afterwards, not shaken with the mixture. Minnehaha is the Indian (U.S.A.) for "Laughing Water."

Nick's Own

Fill the bar glass half full of broken ice and add:

1 dash of Angostura Bitters.
1 dash of Absinthe.
¼ gill of Cognac Brandy.
¼ gill of Italian Vermouth.

Stir up well, strain into a cocktail-glass, and add cherry and lemon-peel squeezed on top.

(Recipe by A. Nicholls, London, 1922.)

Old-Fashioned Cocktail

Put a piece of sugar in a tumbler with a strong bottom and soak with Angostura Bitters. Reduce it with a muddler or spoon, add ¾ gill of Rye Whisky and a lump of ice. Stir up and drop a little lemon-peel squeezed in the glass. Serve a glass of iced water (a chaser) at the same time, to drink afterwards.

It should be noted that the old-fashioned cocktail is prepared and served in the same glass.

Olivette Cocktail

The Olivette Cocktail is a London cocktail made with Plymouth Gin instead of London Gin.

Orange Blossom Cocktail

¼ gill of Gin and ¼ gill of Orange Juice iced and well shaken with a little dash of Orange Bitters, and a dash of Grenadine if required sweet.

(Recipe by Malloy of Pittsburg.)

Paradise Cocktail

Fill the shaker half full of broken ice and add:

    ⅛ gill of Orange Juice.
    ⅛ gill of Apricot Brandy.
    ⅛ gill of Gin.

Shake well and strain into a cocktail-glass.

Perfect Cocktail

This cocktail is always well shaken. It is composed of:

$\frac{1}{4}$ gill of Dry Gin.
$\frac{1}{8}$ gill of French Vermouth.
$\frac{1}{8}$ gill of Italian Vermouth.

A piece of orange-peel is squeezed on top; a dash of Absinthe, if required, improves it.

Ping-Pong Cocktail

This is a Manhattan Cocktail, but Sloe Gin is used instead of Rye Whisky.

(*Recipe by Boothby of San Francisco.*)

Princess Mary

Fill the shaker half full of broken ice and add:

$\frac{1}{6}$ gill of Dry Gin.
$\frac{1}{6}$ gill of Crème-de-Cacao.
$\frac{1}{6}$ gill of fresh cream.

Shake well and strain into a cocktail-glass.

Harry, of Ciro's Club, introduced this cocktail in honour of Princess Mary's wedding to Lord Lascelles, February, 1922.

Queen's Cocktail

Smash a slice of orange and pine-apple in the shaker, add ice and

$\frac{1}{6}$ gill of Gin.
$\frac{1}{6}$ gill of French Vermouth.
$\frac{1}{6}$ gill of Italian Vermouth.

Shake well and strain into a cocktail-glass.

(*Recipe by Harry Craddock, New York.*)

R.A.C. Cocktail

Fill the bar glass half full of broken ice and add:

$\frac{1}{4}$ gill of Dry Gin.
$\frac{1}{8}$ gill of French Vermouth.
$\frac{1}{8}$ gill of Italian Vermouth.
1 dash of Grenadine.
1 dash of Orange Bitters.

Stir up well, strain into a cocktail-glass, add a cherry, and squeeze orange-peel on top.

R.A.C. means Royal Automobile Club. This is the largest club in London, with over 16,000 members.

(*Recipe by Fred Faecks*, 1914.)

Rob Roy Cocktail

Fill the large bar glass half full of broken ice and add:

2 or 3 dashes of Gum Syrup or Curaçao.
1 or 2 dashes of Angostura Bitters.
$\frac{1}{4}$ gill of Scotch Whisky.
$\frac{1}{4}$ gill of French Vermouth.

Stir up well, strain into a cocktail-glass, add a cherry, and squeeze lemon-peel on top.

Rose Cocktail

Fill the bar glass half full of broken ice and add:

3 dashes of Grenadine.
$\frac{1}{4}$ gill of Dry Gin.
$\frac{1}{8}$ gill of French Vermouth.
$\frac{1}{8}$ gill of Dubonnet.

Stir up well, strain into a cocktail-glass, add a cherry, and squeeze lemon-peel on top.

Sidney Knight, the famous bar-tender of the

Hotel Cecil in London, introduced this cocktail in London at the Alhambra Theatre many years ago.

Royal Cocktail

Fill the bar glass half full of broken ice and add:

1 dash of Orange Bitters.
1 dash of Angostura Bitters.
$\frac{2}{8}$ gill of Gin.
$\frac{1}{8}$ gill of Dubonnet.

Stir up well, strain into a cocktail-glass, add a cherry, and squeeze lemon-peel on top. This drink is called Royal because it was first introduced at the Royal Hotel in Dieppe, 1921.

San Martin Cocktail

This well-known South American drink must be well shaken. It contains no Bitters of any description, but:

$\frac{1}{4}$ gill of Gin.
$\frac{1}{4}$ gill of Italian Vermouth.
1 teaspoonful of Yellow Chartreuse.

A little lemon-peel is squeezed on top.

Sensation

Fill the shaker half full of broken ice and add:

3 dashes of Maraschino.
3 sprigs of fresh mint.
$\frac{1}{8}$ gill of Lemon Juice.
$\frac{1}{8}$ gill of Dry Gin.

Shake well and strain into a cocktail-glass.

(Recipe by James Berkelmans, Paris.)

" 75 " Cocktail

Fill the shaker half full of broken ice and add:

2 dashes of Grenadine.
1 teaspoonful of Lemon Juice.
⅛ gill of Calvados.
⅜ gill of Dry Gin.

Shake well and strain into a cocktail-glass.

This cocktail was very well appreciated in Paris during the war. It has been called after the famous light French field gun, and was introduced by Henry of Henry's bar fame in Paris.

Side-Car

Fill the shaker half full of broken ice and add:

⅓ gill of fresh Lemon Juice.
⅓ gill of Cointreau.
⅓ gill of Cognac Brandy.

Shake well and strain into a cocktail-glass.

This cocktail is very popular in France. It was first introduced in London by MacGarry, the celebrated bar-tender of Buck's Club.

Silver Cocktail

Fill the bar glass half full of broken ice and add:

3 or 4 dashes of Maraschino.
2 dashes of Orange Bitters.
¼ gill of Gin.
¼ gill of French Vermouth.

Stir up well, strain into a cocktail-glass, and add squeezed lemon-peel on top.

Silver Streak

Fill the shaker half full of broken ice and add:

¼ gill of Kümmel.
¼ gill of Dry Gin.

Shake well and strain into a cocktail-glass.

Spanish Cocktail

The Spanish Cocktail, or Spanish Delight, is shaken until frothy. The ingredients are:

4 strong dashes of Angostura Bitters.
½ gill of Italian Vermouth.

Before straining into the cocktail-glass squeeze the essence of 3 or 4 pieces of lemon-peel in the glass. Pour the mixture into the glass and drop another piece of squeezed lemon-peel into the glass.

The name of this cocktail is well chosen, because it suits the taste of the Spanish-speaking people of Europe and America.

Star Cocktail

A Klondyke Cocktail with 2 dashes of Orange Curaçao in it.

Stinger Cocktail

Fill the shaker half full of broken ice and add:

⅙ gill of Peppermint.
⅔ gill of Old Brandy.

Shake well and strain into a cocktail-glass. Some people think a dash of Absinthe improves this drink.

Sunshine Cocktail

This favourite concoction of the famous Olympia Club at 'Frisco contains:

2 dashes of Orange Bitters.
$\frac{1}{6}$ gill of Old Tom Gin.
$\frac{1}{6}$ gill of French Vermouth.
$\frac{1}{6}$ gill of Italian Vermouth.

Stir up well, strain into a cocktail-glass, and add lemon-peel squeezed on top.

Thistle Cocktail

Fill the bar glass half full of broken ice and add:

2 dashes of Angostura Bitters.
$\frac{1}{6}$ gill of Italian Vermouth.
$\frac{2}{6}$ gill of Scotch Whisky.

Stir up well, strain into a cocktail-glass and squeeze lemon-peel on top.

This cocktail is also called "York Cocktail."

Turf Cocktail

Fill the bar glass half full of broken ice and add:

2 dashes of Orange Bitters.
2 dashes of Maraschino.
2 dashes of Absinthe.
$\frac{1}{4}$ gill of Plymouth Gin.
$\frac{1}{4}$ gill of French Vermouth.

Stir up well, strain into a cocktail-glass, add olive.

Note especially no squeezed lemon-peel on top.

(Recipe by Harry Johnson, New Orleans.)

Tuxedo Cocktail

A Tuxedo is a Silver Cocktail made with Burnett Gin and including a dash of Absinthe.

Tipperary

Fill the shaker half full of broken ice and add:

1 teaspoonful of fresh Orange Juice.
1 teaspoonful of Grenadine.
2 sprigs of tender mint.
$\frac{1}{6}$ gill of Italian Vermouth.
$\frac{2}{6}$ gill of Gin.

Shake well and strain into a cocktail-glass.

Trocadero

Fill the bar glass half full of broken ice and add:

1 dash of Orange Bitters.
1 dash of Grenadine.
$\frac{1}{4}$ gill of French Vermouth.
$\frac{1}{4}$ gill of Italian Vermouth.

Stir up well, strain into a cocktail-glass, add a cherry, and squeeze lemon-peel on top.

(*Recipe of the Bremen Trocadero*, 1910.)

Vanderbilt Cocktail

Fill the large bar glass half full of broken ice and add:

3 dashes of Gum Syrup.
2 dashes of Angostura Bitters.
$\frac{1}{4}$ gill of Old Brandy.
$\frac{1}{4}$ gill of Cherry Brandy Rocher.

Stir up well and strain into a cocktail-glass, add a cherry and lemon-peel squeezed on top.

This drink was first made at the Kursaal in Ostend during a visit of Colonel Cornelius Vanderbilt, the American millionaire, who was drowned on the *Lusitania* during the war.

Velocity Cocktail

This drink is similar to the H.P.W., but the proportions of the ingredients are reversed. The "Velocity" contains a slice of orange and $\frac{2}{3}$ gill of Gin, and $\frac{1}{3}$ gill of Italian Vermouth. Well shaken and strained into a cocktail-glass.

Ward Eight Cocktail

This cocktail must be well shaken. It is composed of:

1 teaspoonful of Grenadine.
$\frac{1}{8}$ gill of Orange Juice.
$\frac{1}{8}$ gill of Lemon Juice.
$\frac{1}{4}$ gill of Rye Whisky.

This cocktail originates from Boston (U.S.A.), a city divided into eight wards.

Wax Cocktail

Fill up a bar glass half full of broken ice and add:

3 dashes of Orange Bitters.
$\frac{1}{2}$ gill of Plymouth Gin.

Stir up well, strain into a cocktail-glass, add cherry, and squeeze a little orange-peel on top.

This drink is well known in Vancouver and also in British Columbia.

Whip Cocktail

This cocktail is well known amongst the naval officers of the Mediterranean Squadron. The ingredients are:

⅛ gill of Absinthe Pernod.
⅛ gill of French Vermouth.
⅛ gill of Brandy.
⅛ gill of Curaçao.

Shake until frozen.

In Egypt they call it "Kurbag," which is the Arabic word for whip.

White Cocktail

Fill the bar glass half full of broken ice and add:

2 dashes of Orange Bitters.
2 teaspoonfuls of Anisette.
½ gill of Dry Gin.

Stir up well, strain into a cocktail-glass, add olive, and squeeze lemon-peel on top.

(*Recipe by Harry Brecker, Antwerp.*)

Whiz-Bang

Fill the bar glass half full of broken ice and add:

2 dashes of Orange Bitters.
2 dashes of Grenadine.
2 dashes of Absinthe.
⅙ gill of French Vermouth.
⅜ gill of Scotch Whisky.

Stir up well and strain into a cocktail-glass. Squeeze lemon-peel on top.

(*Recipe by Tommy Burton, Sports' Club, London* 1920.)

This cocktail is named after the high-velocity

shells, so called by the "Tommies" during the war, because all you heard was a whiz and the explosion of the shell immediately afterwards.

X.Y.Z.

This cocktail is made exactly like the Bronx, but Lemon Juice is used instead of Orange Juice, and a little plain Syrup or Gomme is added to sweeten the cocktail.

Yellow Parrot Cocktail

This Boston drink is made of:

⅛ gill of Absinthe.
⅛ gill of Yellow Chartreuse.
⅛ gill of Apricot Brandy.

Shake well and strain into a cocktail-glass.

Yellow Rattler Cocktail

This Cowboys' Cocktail is similar to the Cooperstown Cocktail, but a small bruised white onion is used instead of the bruised fresh mint sprigs.

NON-ALCOHOLIC COCKTAILS

Amber Cocktail

CUT a few white grapes in halves, take out the seeds, cut some pine-apple into slices and also some apple; mix with lemon juice and add Pine-apple Syrup according to taste; ice well until the fruit flavours are well blended. Serve in sherbet glass.

Note.—A sherbet glass is like a small tumbler, holding about ¾ gill. It is usually served on a small dish or plate surrounded with shaved ice to keep its contents thoroughly cold.

Apricot Cocktail

Cut up a few apricots, add a little Apricot Syrup, a dash of lemon juice, cubes of pine-apple, grapes, banana. Cover with whipped cream and grated dry nuts. Serve well iced in sherbet glass.

Florida Cocktail

Fill the shaker half full of broken ice and add:
    The juice of a lemon.
    The juice of half an orange.
    3 dashes of Angostura Bitters.
    1 or 2 dashes of Gum Syrup if required, sweet.
Shake well and strain into a small wine-glass.

Jersey Cocktail

Fill the bar glass half full with broken ice and add:
    3 dashes of Gum Syrup.
    1 or 2 dashes of Angostura Bitters.
    1 wine-glass of non-alcoholic Cider.
Stir up well, strain into a wine-glass, add a cherry, and squeeze lemon-peel on top.

Lobster Cocktail

Prepare a sauce of tomato catsup, a little grape fruit juice, and lemon juice. Add salt, paprika, and a little Worcester sauce. Drop chopped pieces of cold lobster in this mixture and serve in sherbet glass surrounded by ice.

In London some reputed *maîtres d'hôtels* add a little cream and generally a little vinegar instead of the grape fruit juice.

The Oyster, Crab, and Shrimp Cocktails are prepared in the same way.

Pussyfoot Cocktail

This is the author's own recipe in admiration for plucky Pussyfoot Johnson, the world's total abstainers' champion.

Fill a shaker half full of broken ice and add:

The juice of 1 lemon.
The juice of 1 orange.
A little plain syrup or apricot syrup.
3 sprigs of mint.
A little white of egg.

Shake well and strain into a small wine-glass.

Rose Cocktail

Fill the shaker half full of broken ice and add:

3 or 4 strawberries cut in pieces.
Half a slice of pine-apple cut in pieces.
The juice of half a lemon.
The juice of 1 orange.
A few dashes of *fleur d'oranger*.

Sweeten to taste with any fruit syrup. Shake well, strain into a small wine-glass, and decorate with rose petals.

Summer Cocktail

Mash to a pulp a few currants, raspberries, and strawberries with bar sugar. Strain the juice very carefully into the shaker, half filled with broken ice, add a little lemon juice and the same quantity of water. Shake well and strain into a small wine-glass.

Tomato Cocktail

Put a nice ripe tomato for 1 or 2 minutes in hot water. This will make it easy to take the skin off. Now put into a sherbet glass alternatively 1 slice of tomato and 1 slice of orange without the peel. Cover with a sauce composed of orange juice, a little tarragon vinegar, and olive oil. Sprinkle with chopped parsley, and serve well iced.

Vegetable Cocktail

Use cooked spring vegetables, chopped very small, mix like a salad with oil, vinegar, salt, pepper, and fine herbs. Serve in sherbet glass surrounded by ice.

COBBLERS

THE Cobblers are long drinks and very refreshing during the hot weather. They can be made with almost any kind of wines, and also with Whisky, Gin, Brandy, etc.

Sherry Cobbler

In the old days this drink used to be prepared and served in the same glass. Now it is generally prepared in the shaker or in the mixing glass.

The ingredients are:

1 teaspoonful of Sugar Syrup.
1 teaspoonful of Pine-apple Syrup (American style) or Curaçao (French style).
1 gill of Sherry.

Well iced and shaken or stirred up. Strain into a tumbler which has been filled with broken ice beforehand. Decorate the top neatly with slices of fruit in season, and pour a little Port on top. Serve with straws and a spoon.

Champagne Cobbler

The Champagne Cobbler must be stirred up gently. No Port is poured on top, but a little lemon juice mixed with it improves it.

Coffee Cobbler

The base liquor is Old Brandy.

Tea Cobbler

The base liquor is Old Jamaica Rum.

COOLERS

THE name of these long drinks describes the effect they produce on those that consume them.

Some are made with liquors; others are absolutely non-alcoholic drinks.

Boston Cooler

Put in a large tumbler the whole peel of a lemon, a lump of ice, with equal parts of Sarsaparilla and Ginger Ale. Serve and drink when fizzy.

Brunswick Cooler

In a large tumbler put:
The strained juice of a lemon.
1 teaspoonful of Sugar Syrup.
1 or 2 lumps of ice, and add cold Ginger Ale.
Stir up carefully and serve.

Bull Dog

Put a big lump of ice into a large tumbler. Add:
The juice of half a lemon.
¾ gill of Dry Gin.
A little Sugar Syrup (if desired sweet).
Fill up with iced Belfast Ginger Ale.
Stir up carefully and serve.

Cablegram

Use Rye Whisky instead of Gin, as in the Bull Dog.

Hara-kiri

The Hara-kiri is a Whisky sour strained into a large tumbler, and the balance is filled up with cold Vichy water.

This drink is usually decorated with fruits in season cut in slices. Serve with a spoon.

Remsen Cooler

A Remsen Cooler is made like the Bull Dog, but Remsen's Scotch Whisky is used instead of Gin.

Rocky Mountain Cooler

Fill the shaker half full of broken ice and add:

The whole of a fresh egg.
Sugar Syrup according to taste.
The juice of a lemon.

Shake well and strain into a tumbler, fill up the balance with cold Cider and grate a little nutmeg on top.

Saratoga Cooler

A Saratoga Cooler is a Brunswick Cooler made with fresh lime juice instead of lemon juice.

Tod's Cooler

In a large tumbler put:

The juice of half a lemon.
$\frac{1}{2}$ gill of Dry Gin.
$\frac{1}{8}$ gill of Cassis de Dijon.
1 or 2 lumps of ice.
Fill up with cold Soda.
Stir up gently and serve.

This drink was very popular in racing circles in the summer of 1910 in Ostend and Brussels, and during the following winter on the Riviera. It was first introduced by the once-famous jockey, Tod Sloan, at the Palace Hotel, Brussels, 1910.

Zenith Cooler

Smash a thick slice of fresh pine-apple and strain the juice carefully into a large tumbler. Add Sugar Syrup according to taste, $\frac{3}{4}$ gill of Gin, 2 lumps of ice. Fill up the glass with cold Soda Water. Stir up and serve with a piece of pine-apple in the glass.

CRUSTAS

THE Crustas are generally made with Gin, Whisky, Brandy, or Rum, and are therefore called accordingly, that is to say, when Gin is used as the base liquor, it is called a Gin Crusta.

Always remember that the Crusta glass, a small wine-glass, should be prepared before the mixture in the following way:

Moisten the edges with lemon, and dip the glass in pulverised sugar. Cut the ends of a clean lemon, peel the rest like an apple, and put this peel in the wine-glass so that it lines the whole inside of the glass.

To prepare the **Gin Crusta** fill the shaker half full of broken ice and add:

3 dashes of Gum Syrup.
3 dashes of Maraschino.
2 dashes of Angostura Bitters.
The juice of a quarter of a lemon.
½ gill of Gin.

Shake well, strain into a Crusta glass, and add a few slices of fruit. Serve with a spoon.

St. Croix Crusta.

A Rum Crusta, but use St. Croix Rum only.

CUPS

THERE are many kinds of Cups. I will only explain here how to prepare several refreshing Cups for luncheon and dinner. The ingredients are for a party of four people.

Champagne Cup

Put a large lump of ice in a big jug and add:

1 liqueur glass of Abricotine.
1 liqueur glass of Curaçao.
2 liqueur glasses of Brandy.
1 bottle of iced Champagne.
1 bottle of cold Soda Water.

Stir up well and decorate with different kinds of fruit in season. A sprig of fresh mint or borage, or even a slice of cucumber-peel, are often added.

Cider Cup

Put a large piece of ice in a big jug and add:

1 gill of Pale Sherry.
½ gill of Brandy.
¼ gill of Curaçao.
2 pint bottles of the best Cider.
The rind of a whole lemon.

Stir up and serve.

Claret Cup

The Claret Cup is made in the same way as the Champagne Cup, but a little Lemon Juice instead of Abricotine improves it.

Dancer's Cup

Put a large lump of ice into a big jug and add 1 liqueur glass of Orgeat Syrup. Fill the jug with equal parts of the best iced Cider and cold Soda Water. Stir up well, and decorate with thin slices of lemon.

A wine-glass of Old Brandy improves this Cup tremendously.

Hock Cup

A delicious Hock Cup is made in a similar way as the before-mentioned Champagne Cup by substituting Hock for Champagne and omitting the Abricotine.

Madeira Cup

Put a large piece of ice in a big jug and add:

The juice of a lemon.

½ gill of Mandarinette.

1 bottle of Dry Madeira Wine.

1 bottle of cold Soda Water.

Stir up well and decorate with thinly cut slices of lemon and a little borage.

Orange Cup

This Temperance Cup is very good. In a large jug put a big lump of ice, add 1 pint of strained fresh orange juice and the juice of 1 lemon to give it a tang. Sweeten with ½ gill of Sugar Syrup and ½ gill of Apricot Syrup. Fill the jug up with iced water or equal parts of water and Soda Water. Decorate with thinly cut slices of oranges, after having stirred these ingredients up well.

This Cup is very much appreciated at dances and garden parties.

Peace Cup

Smash 3 or 4 slices of fresh pine-apple and also two dozen clean strawberries, add some castor sugar and a little water. Strain very carefully into a large jug, add a big lump of ice, and ½ gill of Maraschino, a bottle of dry iced Champagne, and a bottle of cold Soda Water. Stir up well and decorate with pieces of pine-apple cut into dice and little strawberries.

DAISIES

DAISIES are delicious drinks, but they should be made carefully. The best known are those prepared with Gin, Rum, Whisky, etc.

Here is a recipe for a

Morning Glory Daisy

The Morning Glory Daisy is made of the following ingredients:
    The white of a fresh egg.
    The juice of half a lemon.
    1 teaspoonful of Sugar Syrup.
    ½ gill of Gin, Whisky, or Brandy, according
        to taste.
    3 dashes of Absinthe.
Ice well and shake. Strain into a wine-glass.

Rum Daisy

Dissolve a little sugar and water in the shaker, add ice, the juice of half a lemon, ⅛ gill of Curaçao or Yellow Chartreuse, and ½ gill of Rum.

Shake well and strain into a wine-glass. Decorate the top with fruit cut in slices. Serve with a spoon.

Note.—Some bar-tenders serve the daisies in a tumbler, which they then fill up with cold soda water.

EGG NOGGS

EGG NOGGS are very nourishing. They invariably contain fresh eggs and milk, and can be served iced, or hot by using boiling milk instead of the ice and cold milk.

Plain Egg Nogg

Fill the shaker half full of broken ice and add:

1 fresh egg.
1 teaspoonful of Sugar Syrup.
¼ gill of Brandy, Rum, Gin, Whisky, etc., according to taste.
The balance rich milk.

Shake well and strain into a tumbler. Add grated nutmeg on top.

Egg Nogg

The egg nogg is made in the same way, but the base liquors are:

½ gill of Brandy.
¼ gill of Rum.

It is therefore slightly stronger than the plain egg nogg.

Baltimore Egg Nogg

This egg nogg is stronger than the usually prepared egg noggs because it contains:

A fresh egg.
1 teaspoonful of Sugar Syrup.
1 gill of Madeira.
¼ gill of Brandy.
¼ gill of Jamaica Rum.

Shake up with fresh milk and strain into a large tumbler with grated nutmeg on top.

Breakfast

This egg nogg used to be very popular amongst the regular customers of the Criterion American Bar in London some years ago. The ingredients are:

1 fresh egg.
¼ gill of Orange Curaçao.
½ gill of Old Brandy.
Balance rich milk.

Ice well, shake, and strain into a tumbler. Grate cinnamon on top.

General Harrison's Egg Nogg

This drink is very old and well known throughout the southern part of the U.S.A. It is non-alcoholic, and made exactly like the Rocky Mountain Cooler.

FIZZES

FIZZES are very good drinks in the morning. They should be drunk as soon as they are ready because they lose their flavour very quickly.

Cream Fizz

A Cream Fizz is a Gin Fizz to which a little cream has been added.

Gin Fizz

Fill the shaker half full of broken ice and add:
   A teaspoonful of Sugar Syrup.
   The juice of one lemon.
   Three-quarters of a gill of Gin.

Shake well, strain into a tumbler, and fill up with cold Soda Water. Serve and drink immediately.

Golden Fizz

A Golden Fizz is a Gin Fizz to which the yolk of a fresh egg has been added.

Morning Glory Fizz

Fill the shaker half full of broken ice and add:
   The white of a fresh egg.
   Sugar Syrup according to taste.
   The juice of half a lemon or equal parts Lime
      and Lemon Juice.
   3 dashes of Absinthe.
   ¾ gill of Gin, Whisky or Brandy, as required.

Shake well, strain into a tumbler, and fill up with cold Soda Water.

The author recommends this drink as a nerve settler.

5

Orange Fizz

The Orange Fizz is a Gin Fizz, but Orange Juice is substituted for Lemon Juice.

Royal Fizz

A Royal Fizz is a Gin Fizz with the whole of an egg in it. Sometimes Grenadine is substituted for the Sugar Syrup.

Silver Fizz

A Gin Fizz with the white of an egg in it.

Texas Fizz

Fill the shaker half full of broken ice and add:

The juice of half a lemon.
The same amount of Orange Juice.
A little Grenadine to sweeten, according to taste.
¾ gill of Gin.

Shake well, strain into a tumbler, and fill up with cold Soda Water.

FLIPS

THE Flips belong to the same class of drinks as the egg noggs, but contain the yolk of a fresh egg and never any milk. They can be made of Port, Sherry, Claret, Gin, Dubonnet, fruit juices, etc.

Ale Flip
The Ale Flip is a very old drink made of the yolk of an egg beaten up with sugar and Ale. It can be made with or without ice, or served hot by heating the Ale. When shaken, the Ale used should not contain gas, therefore use Bitter Ale. Always grate nutmeg on top.

Boston Flip
The base liquors for the Boston Flip are ¼ gill of Madeira and ¼ gill of Rye Whisky.

Champagne Flip
The best way to make a Champagne Flip is by thoroughly shaking the yolk of a fresh egg with ice. Then open the shaker and add the Champagne. Strain into a wine-glass and grate nutmeg on top. Sugar or Sugar Syrup is only added when required sweet.

Lemon Flip
The Lemon Flip is similar to the Sherry Flip, but fresh Lemon Juice is used instead of Sherry.

Sherry Flip

Fill the shaker half full of broken ice and add:

> The yolk of a fresh egg.
> Sugar Syrup according to taste.
> ½ gill of Dry Pale Sherry.

Shake well, strain into a small wine-glass, and add grated nutmeg on top.

FRAPPÉS

"FRAPPÉ" is the French word for "well-iced" and is used when referring to wines or liqueurs.

Brooklyn Kümmel

Fill a small wine-glass full of fine shaved ice, and add on top a slice of lemon. Pour the kümmel over it.

At St. Moritz, in Switzerland, the *Cut Kümmel* is very familiar. It is a Kümmel Frappé with a dash of Scotch Whisky on top.

Champagne Frappé

The Champagne bottle is put into a silver cooler, surrounded by ice, and left until thoroughly cold. Usually freezing salt is added to hasten the cooling.

Liqueurs Frappées

All liqueurs can be "frappée." This way of drinking liqueurs is generally adopted in the fashionable restaurants on the Continent in the summer after dinner parties. The required liquor is poured into a cocktail-glass which has been filled up with fine shaved ice, and a pair of small straws are served with it.

FRENCH APÉRITIFS

THE "apéritifs," or French Appetisers, are served before luncheon and dinner. They are long drinks, and usually served with cold water or Soda Water.

The best known are:

Dubonnet-Citron

The ingredients are:

½ gill of Dubonnet.
⅛ gill Sirop de Citron.
Balance Soda Water and ice.

Byrrh, Bannuyls, Kina Lillet, etc., are also used instead of Dubonnet.

Picon-Grenadine

The ingredients are:

½ gill of Amer Picon.
⅛ gill of Grenadine.
Balance Soda Water and ice.

Grenadine is often replaced by Curaçao, Sirop de Gomme, Sirop de Citron.

Polichinelle or Cassis-Kirsch

The ingredients are:

½ gill of Cassis de Dijon.
⅛ gill of Kirsch.
Balance Soda Water and a lump of ice.

Chambéry-Fraisette

The ingredients are:

½ gill of Vermouth Chambéry.
⅛ gill of Fraisette Cornu (Strawberry Syrup).
Balance Soda and ice.

Vermouth Curaçao

Put a lump of ice in a tumbler and add:

½ gill of French Vermouth.
⅛ gill of Curaçao.
The balance cold water or Soda Water.

When Cassis is used instead of Curaçao, the drink is called *Export Cassis*. Bitter Français, Bitter Secrestat, etc., are also used instead of French Vermouth, and the apéritif is then called Bitter Curaçao, Secrestat Curaçao.

HIGHBALLS

THE highballs are usually made with Gin, Whisky, Rum, Vermouth, Sherry, Dubonnet, etc., and are then called "Straight Highballs."

The non-alcoholic highballs are prepared in the same way by using any kind of fruit syrup instead of the above-mentioned liquors.

Bizzy Izzy Highball

The base liquor is ¼ gill of Rye Whisky and ¼ gill of Pale Sherry. A little Lemon Juice, sweetened to taste, and cold Soda Water.

Kitty

Is a Claret and Ginger Ale Highball.

Straight Scotch Highball

Put 2 or 3 lumps of ice in a tumbler, ¾ gill of Scotch Whisky, and fill up with cold Soda Water. Some people also like a slice of lemon or a little lemon-peel in it, but this is a matter of taste.

Raspberry Highball

Use ½ gill of Raspberry Syrup, 2 or 3 lumps of ice, and cold Soda. A little Lemon Juice improves this drink.

LEMONADES

American Lemonade

Is a Lemon Squash, but ¼ gill of Port is added on top.

Claret Lemonade

Is a Lemon Squash filled up with equal parts of Claret and cold Soda Water.

Fruit Lemonade

A delicious fruit lemonade is made with ½ gill of Lemon Juice, ½ gill of Orange Juice, Grenadine to sweeten according to taste, 2 or 3 sprigs of mint. Well shaken and strained into a tumbler. Fill the balance up with non-alcoholic Cider.

Lemon Squash

Put into a tumbler the juice of a strained lemon, add Sugar Syrup according to taste, 2 or 3 lumps of ice and cold Soda. Stir up and serve with straws and a slice of lemon on top.

Orange Squash

Orange Squash, or Orangeade, is made like Lemon Squash, but Orange Juice used instead of Lemon Juice.

Orangette

Orangette is an Orange Squash shaken up with a little egg beaten up and cold water.

JULEPS

THE juleps are known in all parts of the world, but they are more popular in the Southern States of the U.S.A. than anywhere else. The best one is the:

Mint Julep

Dissolve 4 or 5 tender sprigs of mint with sugar and water until the flavour of the mint is well extracted. Strain very carefully into the bar glass, add ice and ¾ gill of Old Brandy. Stir up well and strain into a Mint Julep glass prepared in advance. Dash a little rum on top and serve with straws.

The Mint Julep glass is always prepared before the mixture. One can use a tumbler or a large balloon wine-glass, filled with fine shaved ice. Insert 2 or 3 sprigs of mint with the leaves upwards and which have been dipped into powdered sugar before; decorate tastily with berries, pine-apple, banana, orange, etc., according to the season.

Gin Julep

Is made like the Mint Julep, but use Gin instead of Brandy.

This also applies to the Whisky Julep, Rum Julep, etc.

Champagne Julep

The Champagne Julep, it should always be remembered, does not require to be stirred up as much as the other juleps, otherwise the Champagne would lose its flavour and natural taste.

Put 1 lump of sugar in a tumbler, add 1 or 2 sprigs of mint and press them gently with a spoon to extract the mint flavour; add 1 or 2 lumps of ice and pour in the Champagne, stirring carefully at the same time.

Dress with fruit in season and serve.

Old Georgia Julep

Dissolve a little sugar and water in a tumbler; add ½ gill of Brandy and ½ gill of Peach or Apricot Brandy, 3 or 4 tender sprigs of mint, a few lumps of ice and stir up carefully.

This is the real method of mixing a Southern Mint Julep. Mint should not be crushed, and Black Brandy should be used, but Whisky may be substituted if required.

POUSSE CAFÉS

THE "Pousse Cafés" are usually served after luncheon or dinner. They are French drinks and not only popular in France, but all over the Continent and America. There are several liqueurs required in the preparation of these drinks and they must be perfectly separated from each other. The best way to do this is by pouring each liqueur into a different cocktail-glass and then starting with the heaviest liqueurs first, into the Pousse Café glass. Some experts pour the liqueurs from the bottle into a teaspoon and then slowly into the glass along the side.

A Pousse Café may have many liqueurs or only 2 or 3 different ones.

Pousse Café Américain

The ingredients are poured out into the Pousse Café glass in the following order and quantities:

1 teaspoonful of Raspberry Syrup.
⅙ of the capacity of the Pousse Café glass of Maraschino de Zara.
⅙ of the capacity of the Pousse Café glass of green Crème de Vanille.
⅙ of the capacity of the Pousse Café glass of red Curaçao Fockink.
⅙ of the capacity of the Pousse Café glass of Yellow Chartreuse.
⅙ of the capacity of the Pousse Café glass of Old Brandy.

This Pousse Café is also called a "*Rainbow*," because of the similarity of its colours.

Golden Slipper

The Golden Slipper is a South American Pousse Café, well known in Buenos Ayres. It contains:

The yolk of a fresh egg.
⅙ gill of Yellow Chartreuse.
⅙ gill of Eau de Vie de Dantzig, that is Dantziger Goldwasser.

Jersey Lily

Equal parts of Brandy and Yellow Chartreuse. The latter being the heaviest liqueur should be poured out first, the Brandy floating on the top of it.

Knickerbein

This Pousse Café is a favourite drink in Germany. It includes:

The yolk of a fresh egg.
⅙ gill of Dry Orange Curaçao.
⅙ gill of Kümmel Wolfschmidt.
2 dashes of Angostura Bitters on top.

Pousse Café Parisien

The ingredients are:

⅕ of the Pousse Café glass of Sirop de Framboise.
⅕ of the Pousse Café glass of Marasquin de Zara.
⅕ of the Pousse Café glass of Curaçao rouge Rocher.
⅕ of the Pousse Café glass of Chartreuse Jaune.
⅕ of the Pousse Café glass of Fine Champagne.

Pousse l'Amour

Pour in the Pousse Café glass without mixing:

A few dashes of Grenadine.
The yolk of a fresh egg.
⅛ gill of Maraschino.
⅛ gill of Fine Champagne.

This drink should be taken in one gulp.

PUNCHES

PUNCHES are numerous and vary. They can be served either hot or cold. When served cold they are generally decorated with fruits in season, when served hot a slice of lemon on top is sufficient.

Champagne Punch

Fill the shaker half full of broken ice, add 1 tablespoonful of Sugar Syrup, the juice of half a lemon, and 1 tablespoonful of Curaçao. Shake well, strain into a wine-glass and fill up with iced Dry Champagne. Decorate with fruit in season. Serve with a spoon.

Dragoon Punch

This Punch is a favourite drink in the Northern countries of Europe, principally in Sweden and Norway. Here is the recipe for a party of four people:

½ gill of Brandy.
½ gill of Dry Sherry.
A small bottle of Stout.
A small bottle of Lager Beer.
1 bottle of Champagne.

Sweeten according to taste and decorate with thin slices of lemon.

This Punch is usually prepared in a big bowl, and the mixture must be well iced.

Milk Punch

Fill the shaker half full of broken ice and add:

1 tablespoonful of Sugar Syrup.
¼ gill of Rum.
½ gill of Brandy.
Balance rich milk.

Shake well and strain into a tumbler, with nutmeg grated on top.

Planter's Punch

This drink is very popular on the island of Jamaica and principally at Kingston. It is made of:

1 tablespoonful of Sugar Syrup.
The juice of a fresh lime.
1 wine-glass of Bacardi.

Shake well, strain into a tumbler, and grate nutmeg and a pinch of red pepper on top. No soda whatever.

(*Recipe by "Slippery", Myrtle Bank Hotel, Kingston.*)

Rum Punch

Fill the shaker half full of broken ice and add:

1 tablespoonful of plain Syrup or Curaçao.
The juice of half a lemon.
¾ gill of Rum.

Shake well and strain into a wine-glass and add cold Soda Water.

Prince's Punch

This refreshing non-alcoholic Punch is made by boiling five minutes, to extract the flavour, equal quantities of Sugar Syrup and water, together with chopped ginger, a little cinnamon, and a few cloves. Stand until cold and add the juice of 1 lemon and 2 oranges. Put into the shaker with 1 or 2 sprigs of mint and shake, well iced. Pour into the tumbler and decorate with mint and fruit in season. Serve with a spoon.

St. Charles's Punch

The usual quantity of Sugar Syrup and Lemon Juice. A few dashes of Curaçao, $\frac{1}{2}$ gill of Brandy, and $\frac{1}{2}$ gill of Port Wine.

Shake well, strain into a tumbler full of ice, and decorate with fruit. Serve with straw.

This drink is well known in the Southern States of North America.

Tip-Top Punch

The Tip-top Punch is a Brandy Punch filled up with Champagne instead of Soda Water.

6

RICKEYS

RICKEYS are usually taken without sugar and made with fresh limes. The base liquors are Gin, Brandy, Rum, Whisky, Apple Jack, etc.

Here is the recipe for a

Bliz's Royal Rickey

Put 1 or 2 lumps of ice in a tumbler and add:

The juice of half a lime.
The juice of a quarter of a lemon.
1 teaspoonful of Raspberry Syrup.
$\frac{1}{2}$ gill of French Vermouth.
$\frac{1}{4}$ gill of Gin.

Fill up the balance with Ginger Ale, stir up, add fruit on top, and serve with a spoon.

Sloe Gin Rickey

Put 1 or 2 lumps of ice in a tumbler, cut a good-sized lime in half and squeeze the juice in the glass, add $\frac{3}{4}$ gill of Sloe Gin, fill up with cold Soda and serve with a spoon.

SANGAREES

SANGAREES are usually made with Beer or Wines, but also with Gin, Brandy, Rum, etc.

When made with Ale always be careful when pouring out. New Ale is very foamy, and one should prevent the Ale from running over the glass. The Ale should not be too warm or too cold as no ice is used in the

Ale Sangaree

Dissolve a tablespoonful of sugar in a small wine-glass of water. Pour this into a large tumbler, and fill up with Ale. Grate nutmeg on top and serve.

Whisky Sangaree

Is made like the Ale Sangaree, but Scotch or Rye Whisky and water is used instead of Ale. Also put 1 or 2 lumps of ice in the glass.

SLINGS

ALL Slings are made the same way; one has only to substitute the base liquor. When desired cold use water and ice; when hot use boiling water.

Hot Apple Jack Sling

Fill a tumbler half full of boiling water and Sugar Syrup to sweeten, ¼ gill of Apple Jack Brandy or Calvados, and stir up gently. Squeeze the peel of a lemon into the glass, and add grated nutmeg.

Some people prefer a tablespoonful of fresh lemon juice also in it.

Straits Sling

This well-known Singapore drink, thoroughly iced and shaken, contains:

    2 dashes of Orange Bitters.
    2 dashes of Angostura Bitters.
    The juice of half a lemon.
    ⅛ gill of Bénédictine.
    ⅛ gill of Dry Cherry Brandy.
    ½ gill of Gin.

Pour into a tumbler and fill up with cold Soda Water.

SMASHES

ALL Smashes are made the same way by sub-stituting the base liquors.

Gin Smash

Dissolve a little sugar and water in a shaker, add 3 sprigs of mint, press the flavour out of them, and put sprigs aside. Fill the shaker with ice, add ½ gill of Gin, shake and strain into a wine-glass. Dress with fruit and serve with a spoon.

Fancy Gin Smash

Is made in the same way as the plain Gin Smash. The glass is, however, filled up with chipped ice and decorated with fruits and a little sprig of mint. Serve with straws and a spoon.

SOURS

THE Sours are cooling and pleasant drinks. They are generally prepared with Gin, Brandy, Rum Whisky, etc.

Brandy Sour

Fill the shaker half full of broken ice, add a few dashes of plain Syrup, and the juice of half a lemon, ½ gill of Brandy. Shake well and strain into a wine-glass, add a little splash of syphon on top, and decorate with fruit.

A few drops of white of egg improves all Sours.

Continental Sour

Is an ordinary Sour made with Brandy and a dash of Claret on top.

Egg Sour

Substitute a fresh egg for the base liquor.

Victoria Sour

The ingredients are ¼ gill of Whisky and ¼ gill of Sherry, with a dash of Rum and sweetened with equal parts of Pine-apple Syrup and Apricot Syrup.

TODDIES

THESE drinks can be served hot or cold by using respectively hot water or ice and cold water.

Dissolve sugar and water in a small tumbler, put ice in glass, add ½ gill of the liquor desired.

The hot toddies are generally served with a slice of lemon on top. In France they are called "Grogs."

Hot Apple Toddy

Strain the juice of a baked apple, some sugar, and a little hot water into a tumbler, add ¾ gill of Apple Jack Brandy. Fill up with boiling water and add grated nutmeg on top.

VARIOUS DRINKS

American Glory

PUT the juice of half an orange in a tumbler, add 2 lumps of ice, and equal parts of Champagne and Soda Water. Stir up with a spoon and serve.

Black Stripe

Dissolve 1 tablespoonful of honey with a little hot water in a tumbler. When cool add 2 or 3 lumps of ice, ¾ gill of Rum, and cold water. Grate nutmeg on top and serve.

This drink can also be served hot by using boiling water.

Bull's Milk

This well-known Singapore drink includes:
¾ gill of Old Brandy.
Sugar or Sugar Syrup to taste.
1 pint of fresh milk.
Well iced and shaken. Strained into a tumbler with grated nutmeg and cinnamon on top.

Bosom Caresser

Fill the shaker half full of broken ice and add:
The yolk of a fresh egg.
¼ gill of Madeira.
¼ gill of Brandy.
¼ gill of Curaçao.
¼ gill of Grenadine.
Shake well and strain into a wine-glass.

Brace Up

2 dashes of Angostura Bitters.
2 dashes of White Anisette.
The juice of a small lime.
1 fresh egg.
½ gill of Brandy.
Well iced, shaken, and strained into a tumbler.
Fill up with Vichy Water. Sugar or Sugar Syrup
should only be used in this drink if absolutely
necessary to one's taste.

Champagne Pick-me-up

Fill the shaker half full of broken ice and add
the strained juice of half an orange, a few dashes
of Curaçao or Grenadine, ½ gill of Brandy. Shake
well, strain into a wine-glass, and fill up with
Champagne. A dash of Absinthe on top if
required.

Cloudy Sky

This drink is well known in Philadelphia. It is
a Sloe Gin Rickey filled up with Ginger Ale
instead of Soda Water.

Collins

There are two brothers Collins:
John Collins, which is made with Hollands Gin;
and Tom Collins, which is made with Old Tom
Gin. A Collins can also be made with Whisky,
Brandy, Rum, etc., and is then called Whisky
Collins, Brandy Collins, etc.
The best way to prepare a Collins is the old-

fashioned way, by using two glasses. In the first glass, a tumbler, put ¾ gill of the required Gin, 1 lump of ice, fill up the glass with Soda Water, and leave to get cold.

In the second glass dissolve powdered sugar in the juice of a lemon. Then take the ice out of your tumbler, which will leave room to add the sweetened lemon juice. When doing this stir up at the same time, serve quickly, and drink immediately.

Nowadays the Collins is generally made in the shaker with lemon juice, Sugar Syrup, and Gin, well shaken, strained into a tumbler, and filled up with Soda Water.

Eye-Opener

A good Eye-Opener is made with:

A fresh egg.
½ gill of Old Brandy.
⅛ gill of Absinthe.
⅛ gill of Green Crème de Menthe.

Well iced, shaken, and strained into a small wine-glass.

If this drink does not open the eyes, add a small pinch of red pepper on the top. This will do it properly, and give you a glad eye at the same time.

Glühwein

The Glühwein is a German hot Claret Toddy, made as follows:

In a saucepan put 2 lumps of sugar, 1 slice of lemon, 1 piece of cinnamon, and ½ pint of Claret. Boil and serve as hot as possible.

Horse's Neck

Place the peel of a lemon in a tumbler with one end hanging over the top of the glass, add 2 lumps of broken ice, and fill the glass with cold Ginger Ale.

A *Stiff Horse's Neck* is made the same way by adding a dash of Angostura Bitters and ½ gill of Gin, Brandy, Whisky, etc., as required.

Havelock

This well-known Indian and Australian drink is made of ½ gill of Brandy and double this quantity of Ginger Wine, with 1 lump of ice in the glass.

Itchiban

This Chinese egg nogg includes:
  1 fresh egg.
  1 teaspoonful of Crème de Cacao.
  1 teaspoonful of Bénédictine.
  ½ gill of Brandy.
  Balance cold rich milk.

All iced, shaken, and strained into a tumbler with nutmeg grated on top.

Itchiban is the Chinese for Number One.

Kiss-me-quick

Put 2 or 3 lumps of ice in a tumbler, add:
  2 dashes of Angostura Bitters.
  4 dashes of Curaçao.
  ½ gill of Absinthe.

Fill the glass up with cold Soda Water. Stir up and serve with straws.

Lait de Poule

Lait de Poule means "Cock-a-doodle Broth." It is a French egg nogg made with yolks of 2 eggs beaten up with castor sugar, boiling milk, and ½ gill of Brandy or Rum.

Leave it to me

The juice of half a lemon, 1 teaspoonful of Raspberry Syrup, ½ gill of gin. Iced and well shaken. Strain into a wine-glass and add a splash of soda on top.

Long Whistle

Three-quarters of a gill of Brandy or Whisky, a little Sugar Syrup, and hot or cold milk. Nutmeg grated on top.

Lover's Dream

The Lover's Dream is also called a Glasgow Flip. It is a lemon flip served in a tumbler and filled up with Ginger Ale.

Magnolia

Fill the shaker half full of broken ice and add:

> 1 tablespoonful of Sugar Syrup.
> 1 tablespoonful of Curaçao.
> 1 yolk of a fresh egg.
> ½ gill of Brandy.

Shake well, strain into a tumbler, and fill up with iced Champagne.

Maiden's Blush

Fill the shaker half full of broken ice and add:

1 tablespoonful of Grenadine.
2 dashes of Oxygénée.
½ gill of Gin.

Shake well and strain into a small wine-glass.

(Recipe by Mr. Frank Newman, Paris.)

Night-Cap

The ingredients are:

The yolk of a fresh egg.
¼ gill of Anisette.
¼ gill of Curaçao.
¼ gill of Brandy.

Well iced, shaken, and strained into a small wine-glass.

Pick-Me-Up

Put 1 or 2 pieces of ice in a tumbler, add the juice of a lemon, the same quantity of Worcester Sauce, and fill up with Soda. Stir up gently and serve.

This is a good drink when the stomach is in disorder.

Prairie Oyster

The Prairie Oyster, also called Mountain Oyster in America, is made differently in various parts of the world.

Here is a well-known recipe:

2 teaspoonfuls of Worcester Sauce.
2 teaspoonfuls of Brandy.
1 teaspoonful of Vinegar.
1 teaspoonful of Tomato Ketchup.

Mix well, drop the yolk of a fresh egg in the

glass, and add red pepper on top. Some people like a dash of Angostura Bitters in it, others prefer it without Brandy, but they take a plain glass of Sherry immediately afterwards.

Royal Smile

Fill the shaker half full of broken ice and add:

The juice of half a lime.
1 teaspoonful of Grenadine.
½ gill of Dry Gin.
¼ gill of Apple Jack Brandy.

Shake well and strain into a small wine-glass. A little cream improves this drink.

Some bar-tenders also use plain Cider instead of Apple Jack Brandy.

September Morn

The white of an egg, the juice of half a lime, 1 teaspoonful of Grenadine, and ½ gill of Bacardi, well shaken and strained into a small wine-glass.

Hot Spiced Rum

Put into a tumbler 2 or 3 lumps of sugar and dissolve them in a little boiling water, add:

1 gill of Old Jamaica Rum.
1 piece of butter as large as a small walnut.
1 teaspoonful of spices (cinnamon, cloves, nutmeg).

Fill the glass with boiling water. Stir up well and serve.

Stone Fence

A Whisky and Cider with a lump of ice in it, stirred up gently.

Spike Lemonade

A plain cold Lemonade and Whisky. Usually Rye Whisky.

Shandy Gaff

Equal parts Bass Ale and Ginger Ale.

White Lion

The juice of half a lemon.
¼ gill of Raspberry Syrup.
¼ gill of Curaçao.
¾ gill of Rum.
Well shaken and strained into a tumbler filled with chopped ice, and tastily decorated with fruits in season.

INVALID DRINKS

Beef Tea

PUT into a cup a good teaspoonful of meat extract, such as Bovril or Oxo, add a little salt, and fill up with boiling water. Stir up with a spoon.

Occasionally the yolk of a fresh egg is beaten up with the beef tea, which improves it.

Barley Water

Wash properly 2 tablespoonfuls of barley and boil it for 2 hours in 2 quarts of water. Strain it, add sugar to taste, and let it cool.

This drink is nourishing and beneficial to the kidneys.

Egg Drink

Beat up well a fresh egg, add 1 pint of fresh milk, and the same quantity of water whilst stirring it up with a spoon. Sweeten to taste and boil.

This drink relieves sickness of the stomach.

Rice Water

Wash 2 ounces of rice and boil in 2 quarts of water for 90 minutes after adding sugar and grated nutmeg. Rice boiled for a long time becomes gelatinous, and when mixed with milk is an excellent diet.

Sage Tea

Put half an ounce of dried sage leaves in a jar, fill with a quart of boiling water, and add sugar and lemon juice in proportions to suit the patient's taste. This drink is very useful when suffering from fever.

Toast Water

Break a few slices of thin toast in a jar and cover with boiling water. When cold strain and sweeten according to taste. Some patients like the yolk of egg beaten up with it and flavoured with a little grated nutmeg.

DO YOU KNOW THAT—

Aquadiente is a Mexican liqueur made from the *Maquey* aloe. *Pulque Wine* is made from the same.

Araki of Egypt is well known in the Near East, and is a liqueur made from the juice of dates.

Beer. The Germans generally serve beer in Schoppen (a glass covered with a metal top), and it is the custom when drinking with friends to close the metal top. If you forget to do so, they put their glass on the top of your open one and demand another round of beer at your expense.

In Brussels the local beer, called *Gueuze Lambic*, is usually sweetened by adding a lump of sugar or a little grenadine. *Faro* and *Krieken Lambic* are similar to the gueuze lambic, but of inferior quality.

Bee Wine is made from the ginger-beer plant, a fungus which possesses peculiar properties. Although a favourite teetotallers' drink, analysts have proved that it contains more alcohol than beer. It takes a fortnight to brew by placing some of the "bees" in water and adding periodically a little sugar or syrup which produces fermentation. After this it is bottled, laid down for six weeks and is then ready for drinking.

Bismarck is equal parts stout and champagne. In Canada this drink is called *Velvet*.

Brandies. Cognac is the French city where the famous brandies (*Eaux de Vie*) are distilled. They possess a fine taste and an agreeable and delicate aroma. It improves by ageing in the wood.

The *Fine Champagne* are the best brands of cognac brandies. Other well-known brandies are the *Marc de Bourgogne*, the *Armagnac des Pyrénées*, the *Calvados de Normandie* which is made with apples instead of grapes; the *Bacardi of Santiago de Cuba*, a sugar-cane brandy reputed all over the world; the *Fundador*, a famous Spanish brandy; the *Brandy of Odessa*, the *Californian Brandy*, etc.

Apple Jack Brandy, well known in America, is similar to the *Calvados de Normandie*. The *Kamtchatka Watky* is a brandy made of rice. *Brandewyn* is a Dutch brandy; in N. Europe it is known as *Brantwine*.

British Wines. In various parts of Great Britain wine is made from fruits and vegetables, including blackberries, currants, damsons, dandelions, elderberry, orange, parsnip, rhubarb.

Cachiry, from Guiana, is made of sweet potatoes and the *Paya* is very similar to it.

Campari is a bitter made in Italy; it mixes well with vermouth taken with or without water.

Cha is a Chinese fermented beverage made from the sap of the palm tree.

Chambéry is a white French vermouth made in the town which bears that name.

Champagne is a stimulant to the body and mind. Physicians declare that good champagne possesses therapeutic properties. Nelson, Byron, Dickens, and Napoleon I were extremely fond of it. It is of great value to those suffering from dyspepsia, neuralgia, influenza, and gout. It has proved to be a stimulant when no other stimulant can be retained in illness.

There are three kinds of champagne:

Crémant, which is of the best quality and produces a creamy froth.

Mousseux, the next best wine, which is very sparkling and very frothy.

Tisane, which is a "mousseux" of inferior quality.

Champagne was first produced in the seventeenth century and soon became a favourite drink of Louis XIV.

Chicha, from Bolivia, is made of grapes. It is slightly intoxicating.

Cider is the juice of apples, to which is added sugar and water. It contains a little more alcohol than beer, but there are also various brands of non-alcoholic ciders. The best English cider is made with Fair Maid of Devon, Sweet Alfred, and Woodbine Apples, which grow in Devonshire. The best French cider comes from Normandy, while in the U.S.A. the cider of Jersey is famous. Cider improves when matured.

Delphinette is known as the Bénédictine of Grenoble, and the *Génépi des Alpes* the Grand Marnier of the same town.

Dog's Nose is a glass of ale with a dash of gin. It is a popular sailors' drink in the British Navy.

Douzico is a Turkish kind of absinthe, which when taken with water turns white. It has the kümmel taste.

Eau de Vie de Lie. A Swiss liqueur made from the "lie" (the crust which adheres to the wood of the wine casks) is very popular in the Canton de Vaud, Lausanne, and Geneva. The Swiss people are great consumers of this.

Elixir is a liqueur which possesses great qualities. It cures stomach-ache, indigestion, etc. The best known is the *Elixir de Spa*, made in the town of Spa, Belgium, and the *Izarra*, made in the Pyrénées. *Bénédictine, Vieille Cure, Chartreuse* also possess the qualities of good elixir.

Finkel is a spirit like gin, but made from potatoes, of which the Norwegians are very fond. There is a still for making it on every little farm. The Norwegians also produce *Homeburn* or *H.B* from distilled sugar and fermented yeast.

Gin is made of juniper berries. Dry gin contains no sugar; Old Tom Gin has a small percentage of sugar. Sloe gin is gin flavoured with the juice of the sloe berries. *Genièvre* is a gin well known in various European countries; it is made from corn. In Holland this gin is known as *Oude Klaren* or *Schiedam*. In Germany they call it *Schnapps*. *Akavitte* is much stronger than the usual gin; it is made in Denmark, Sweden, and Norway.

Guarapo is a fermented sugar-cane drink of the West Indies.

Guaruzo of Chili is made from rice.

Guignolet de Bourguignon is a kind of cherry brandy made from the *Guigne* (a small black cherry). It is a well-known liqueur in the Dijon district.

Half and Half is a favourite English drink of equal parts ale and stout.

Kava is a Hawaiian liqueur made by the prettiest girls in the villages, called Taupos. In every village there is a taupo. She alone wears the war dress of the men. In war time she is a *vivandière*, carrying food, water, and ammunition, and in peace time she acts as mistress of the ceremonies.

Kava is made by chewing the root of the pepper plant and spitting it into the Kava bowl. The stuff is strained and served in a coco-nut cup. It is also made by beating the root between stones. Too much kava paralyses the legs, but the head remains clear; the drinker becomes emaciated and his skin scaly.

Kwas is a Russian liqueur made of rye.

Lagbi is made in Tripoli from the juice of dates.

Lérina is a delicious liqueur made on the

Lérins Islands, situated in the Mediterranean opposite Cannes.

Mastic is a Greek liqueur well known in the East.

Mescal is a colourless and fiery liqueur obtained by the distillation from the crooked heart of the agave or Mexican aloe.

Mazato of Pérou is made of boiled maize and sugar water.

Navy Rum, known as grog, is one part rum to three parts water.

Pécket is a kind of local gin made from corn in the French-speaking part of Belgium.

Perry is a fermented liquid made from pears, much as cider is made from apples.

Pic à Pou is the local wine of the French Pyrénées.

Pimento Dram of Jamaica is a liqueur invented by the Carib Indians. They have nearly died out and are known as the biggest drunkards in the world. Pimento dram is very strong, but it is a good cure for a cold and fever.

Pinnard is the name given by the French soldiers to the ration wine they receive.

Ponché Soto is a famous liqueur of Spain, and the *Sol y Sombra* (half gin and half Spanish brandy) is a well-known drink of the Spanish sailors. *Sol y Sombra* means "Sun and Shadow." It is the name also given to the seats in the arena at bull-fights.

Saké is the national Japanese beverage. It is usually served in tiny white cups. Seaweed biscuits are served with it.

Schwarzwald Kirschwasser is a German liqueur made of cherries crushed with their stones, and the *Quetsch of Alsace* is a similar liqueur made with prunes.

Secrestat is a famous French bitter. The

Bitter Français, the *Amer Picon,* the Italian *Fernet Branca,* and the Dutch *Boonekamp* are very similar to it.

Sinday is a popular wine in Hindustan, made from the sap of the palm tree.

Slivovitza is known in Austria and Hungary. It is made of fermented prunes.

Strega is a famous Italian liqueur of Milan, and *Trinchieri* and *China Bisleri* are well-known tonic wines.

Striep is a Flemish drink composed of a glass of lager beer, of which half is froth.

Tuica is a Roumanian liqueur made from wild prunes.

Van de Ham is a delicious South African liqueur tasting similar to Bénédictine.

Whisky is made of barley or rye. It has undoubted medicinal value, principally against chill, fever, cold, malaria, fatigue, etc. It is usually stored in sherry casks, which give it a soft and mellow flavour and improve its colour.

The best brands of whisky are distilled in Scotland, Ireland, Canada. There is also a wormwood whisky, made in the neighbourhood of Odessa, which is very popular in the southern parts of Russia. It is called *Polynnaia.*

Wines. The red colour in the wines is due to a pigment contained in the skins of the grapes, which are not removed during the fermentation of the must. In white wines, however, the skins of the grapes are removed.

Practically every country where the climate allows grapes to grow produces wine. Those best known are undoubtedly the French Bordeaux (Claret) and Burgundy wines; the German Hock and Moselle wines; the various Italian, Spanish, Portuguese, Hungarian, Algerian, Madeira, South African, Australian, Californian wines, etc.

The best Burgundy wines are to be found in the Belgian cellars. This is due to the sandy soi which keeps the cellars at a regular temperature.

The German wine saloons, known as "Weins-tüben," possess *Stammtische* (club tables), where friends gather nightly to eat and drink. Fines are paid when drinking wine which costs more than a certain price. This money is saved for dinner parties, and the members also leave in their will a certain amount of money to be spent on wine drunk to their memory.

Yeast, or barm, that mysterious substance, was discovered by Cagnard Latour and Schwann. Pasteur found the various tribes of yeast, which differ as much one from another as Saxons from Zulus. They all possess, however, the power of elaborating alcohol from sugar.

Beer, wines, and spirituous liquors depend for their production entirely on the work of the microbes contained in the yeast.

USEFUL PRESCRIPTIONS

COLD. When the cold is coming on the best way to stop it is to have a hot *toddy* at bed-time or a *Glühwein* (*see recipe*).

When unable to breathe through the nose, dissolve a pinch of powdered borax in hot water, and sniff from the palm of the hand.

A *strong nightcap* at bedtime, say, boiling water with ¾ gill of rum, whisky, or brandy, is very helpful.

To cure a sore throat a *Rock and Rye* is advisable before retiring. This consists of 1 teaspoonful of rock candy syrup, ¾ gill of rye whisky, the juice of half a lemon, and well stirred up. Honey can be used instead of rock candy syrup, but should be dissolved in a little hot water first.

A *Black Stripe* is also good (*see recipe*), or a *Hot Apple Toddy*, prepared by straining the juice of a baked apple, sugar, and a little hot water into a large tumbler; add ¾ gill of apple jack brandy, fill up with boiling water, and grate nutmeg on top.

DIARRHŒA. To cure diarrhœa have a glass of plain blackberry brandy, or if too sweet to your taste mix some old brandy with it.

Another good cure is equal parts of port and brandy with a dash of Angostura.

FEVER. A good remedy against fever, which is generally used in the tropical countries, is equal parts of strong tea and soda water.

HEADACHE. To cure a headache take a little absinthe in the palm of the hand, dry it between the two hands, and sniff through the nose. After this have a plain cocktail with a dash of absinthe or a good *London Cocktail* (*see recipe*) is generally effective.

INDIGESTION. A good cure for indigestion is gin and white peppermint or brandy and green crème de menthe, mixed half and half.

A green crème de menthe and soda is also very relieving.

When suffering just after a meal, take a little bicarbonate of soda and water, or hot black coffee with 1 teaspoonful of glycerine instead of sugar.

INFLUENZA. A good precaution against "flu" is a *hot claret toddy* at bedtime.

Another wonderful mixture is made of:

A fresh egg (the yolk only) beaten up with 1 teaspoonful of lemon or lime syrup, 1 teaspoonful of clove syrup, 1 teaspoonful of cinnamon syrup, and ¾ gill of rum. Put this mixture in a tumbler, add boiling water while stirring up, and drink as hot as possible before going to bed.

NEURALGIA. A mouthful of neat Absinthe Pernod swallowed very slowly will cure neuralgia. Its taste is very strong, but the effect on the pain is radical. Some people prefer old brandy instead.

PICK-ME-UPS. Some liqueurs and certain cocktails mixed properly, and when taken at the right time, possess great medicinal qualities. They can cure slight indispositions, such as colds, stomach trouble, indigestion, neuralgia, etc.

The best way is never to abuse good things; but it happens sometimes unexpectedly that one steps a little over the mark.

Bromo seltzer taken twice within half an hour is undoubtedly a good cure for this indiscretion.

So is a *pick-me-up* of equal parts of lemon juice and Worcester sauce with soda water. Some people believe in lemon juice and soda water only, but this very often causes sickness.

Angostura and soda also produces a good effect. And on the morning after the night before a *Morning Glory Fizz* is helpful. It is a plain fizz made with gin, whisky, brandy, or rum, according to taste, to which the white of an egg has been added and also 3 or 4 dashes of absinthe. That will give one an appetite and quieten the nerves. So will a *Morning Glory Daisy*, which is made exactly in the same way, but without soda.

RHEUMATISM. A good embrocation which stops rheumatism is made with equal quantities of turpentine, olive oil, and whisky or gin. These ingredients should be well shaken until properly mixed, rubbed on the affected part after a hot bath while sitting in front of a good fire. Cover afterwards with a flannel.

SEA-SICKNESS. When feeling uncomfortable while travelling on the sea, lie down and try to sleep and keep the feet warm. Champagne is very effective, and so is lemon juice and soda without sugar.

SLEEPLESSNESS. A good *sleep conducer* is the juice of an orange taken with boiling water. Sugar according to taste and a slice of lemon floating on the top.

Apple tea is also very good. It is made with cut-up apples covered with water and sugar. When boiling strain the juice and drink as hot as possible with grated nutmeg on top. To ensure sleep always remember that the conducer should be taken regularly every night.

The *American Glory* (*see recipe*) is a delicious drink before going to bed, when one has been out late.

STOMACH-ACHE. Very good drinks to soften the pains are half gin and half anisette, half gin and half peppermint, half brandy and half crème de menthe, or half fernet branca bitters and plain water.

Another good prescription is a mixture composed of one liqueur glass full of fernet branca bitters, ditto of white mint, served in a wine-glass and filled up with soda water.

INDEX

CPSIA information can be obtained
at www.ICGtesting.com
Printed in the USA
BVHW080753130620
581406BV00001B/289

9 781614 278320